Nurturing Faith in Families

Nurturing Faith in Families

425 Creative Ideas for Family Ministry

Jolene L. Roehlkepartain

Abingdon Press
Nashville

NURTURING FAITH IN FAMILIES
425 CREATIVE IDEAS FOR FAMILY MINISTRY

Copyright © 2002 by Abingdon Press

This book is printed on acid-free paper.

Library of Congress Cataloging-in-Publication Data

Roehlkepartain, Jolene L., 1962–
  Nurturing faith in families: 425 creative ideas for family
ministry/Jolene L. Roehlkepartain.
      p.   cm.
  Includes bibliographical references and index.
  ISBN 0-687-04921-0 (alk. paper)
  1. Church work with families.   I. Title.

BV4438 .R64 2002
259'.1—dc21

                                                    2001055257

02 03 04 05 06 07 08 09 10 11—10 9 8 7 6 5 4 3 2 1

MANUFACTURED IN THE UNITED STATES OF AMERICA

To Gene,
my husband, who is a true partner in
parenting and a true visionary in the
future of the church

Contents

Foreword

Over the past four years, I have been involved in a research project with thirty-two congregations, an equal mix of National Baptists, Southern Baptists, Presbyterians, and Methodists from four different regions of the country. The research project is studying what families in these congregations are like—their strengths, their stresses and challenges, how they live their faith. In the same week that I began drawing implications for congregational ministry from that research, Jolene Roehlkepartain's manuscript showed up in my mailbox. The coincidence is remarkable. Let me explain.

The families in the congregations we studied were extremely diverse—families with no children, single-parent families, single adults with no children, grandparents raising children, elderly adults and their families—all the diversity that one might imagine in an American congregation today, and then some. Overall, these different types of families showed an amazing level of cohesion, companionship, and ability to handle life stressors. It appears, however, that those families with dependent children and teenagers face the greatest challenges in their life together. It is the presence of children and teenagers—and not the nature of adult relationships in the family—that most predicts that families will struggle more with life challenges than other kinds of families. It is not nearly so significant if the adult in a family is single or married or remarried. What is significant is that there are children in the home. In short, our research indicates that the families that are most vulnerable to stress and challenge, and most likely to have difficulty in living their faith, are families with children.

Nurturing Faith in Families responds to this challenge. Jolene is right; it doesn't take a big budget, or extra staff, or lots of room to minister to families with children. It does take a vision of the church as a community that can help families make sense of the competing demands in their lives, or as she says, "a place of calm in the midst of a daily life that sometimes feels like living in a hurricane." *Nurturing Faith in Families* will help church leaders develop that vision and then make that vision concrete in a mission for the families in their own congregation and community. At no time has this vision been more critical. Several factors are converging with the result that there are fewer and fewer parents in our society: (1) the number of children per family is shrinking, (2) more and more adults are deciding not to or are unable to parent children for various reasons, and (3) even those who do parent are spending at least twice as many life years without dependent children in their homes as those years with children. These trends mean that there are not as many advocates for parents and children as there were in decades past. Of all places in our society, however, parents in church ought not to feel as though they are the only voices speaking on behalf of the needs of their families.

Nurturing Faith in Families makes it clear that nurturing the faith of families with children does not rest solely on parents but, quite the contrary, is the responsibility of the entire congregation. All of us in the community of faith will be enriched by cross-generational and family inclusiveness in our education, our missions and ministry, our congregational care, our music and play, and above all, in our worship. *Nurturing Faith in Families* will provide you with a catalog of ideas and resources for becoming a family faith-nurturing community.

Diana R. Garland, Ph.D.
Editor, *Family Ministry: Empowering Through Faith*
and *AudioMagazine in Family Ministry AM/FM*

Chapter 1

Family Ministry

The critical Ministry of the church

When a church buries more people than it baptizes, it doesn't take long for attendance to drop and budgets to shrink. In order for a congregation to thrive—let alone survive—it needs new life and new energy. The local church needs people who represent the full spectrum of life: from those just starting life to those nearing the end of their lives, as well as all ages in between.

Family ministry is the critical ministry of the church today. Research from the Alban Institute in Bethesda, Maryland,[1] found that a congregation that is "a family place for children" is one of three top benefits newcomers cite as what they look for in a church.[2] In another study, Catholic University sociologist Dean R. Hoge found that 75 percent of Protestants leave the church during the late teen years, but 49 percent return before their late thirties. "Having children is the number-one

About the Term "Family" in This Book

Many churches are redefining the term *family* to mean that everyone (including singles) is in a family. This book focuses on families with children at home, so the term *family* used here refers to families with children and teenagers.

impetus people have for returning to a church," he says.[3]

Because of research on families, more and more churches are starting—or want to start—a family ministry emphasis. Churches know that family ministry is important, but many get stuck because they make one of three major mistakes. First, they don't always know what to do, so they end up doing nothing. Second, they simply try to get families to join without reshaping the ministries of the church. Third, they add programs and activities without first determining how to make all aspects of church life welcoming and nurturing for families.

This book will help you see family ministry as an integral part of congregational life. It gives concrete, practical ideas for how to start a family ministry or to give new life to a program already in existence. The 425 ideas offered here can work in any size church and are presented in a way that allows you to integrate the ones that work best in your setting according to your family ministry vision. This book focuses on what works while highlighting ways to maneuver through common pitfalls so that your family ministry can be an effective part of your overall church ministry and can meet the needs of your families.

What Families Want in a Church

Many churches complain that most families visit once and never come back again. How can a church attract families if families don't stay around long enough to find out what the church is all about?

First impressions can make or break a church. Families tend to look at different aspects of a church than church leaders and long-term members. Imagine a family with an infant, for example. If there is no place for the family to leave the child during worship, the family most likely will not come again. If there is a nursery, but the toys are broken and the care seems haphazard, the family most likely will not return. If no one welcomes the family or asks about the baby, the family often will look for a church somewhere else. If the bathroom doesn't have a place to change a baby, the family may not come back.

This may seem harsh—and unfair. The family hadn't even been to the worship service or the coffee-and-cookies fellowship time. But it's the reality of most families in search of a church home. They're looking for a place that's welcoming to families—in spirit and in design. And *first* impressions make a *big* impression.

Once a family starts visiting a church, Alban Institute researchers say it can take from one month to two years for a family to decide to join.[5] During this time researchers found that it's essential that the returning visiting family feel:

> ## FAST FACT
>
> Changing Families
>
>
>
> Half of all families in 1970 had two parents and children under age eighteen. By 2001 only one-third of all families look like this. In addition, the percentage of single-parent families has almost doubled since 1970.[4]

- accepted and liked by people important to them;

- satisfied with the Sunday school their children attend;

- satisfied with the quality of the clergy[6]

Being accepted and liked by other people in the church is essential for families. In fact, research shows that the first six months is a critical time for families to decide whether or not to join a church. If families find friends quickly, they're much more likely to stick with a church and join it. One of the experts in church growth, Win Arn, found that the more friends people make within six months of starting to attend a church, the more likely they were to join the church. In a study of fifty people, he found the results below.[7]

Number of friends made within six months of coming to the church	Number of those who joined the church
9 or more friends	12
8 friends	12
7 friends	13
6 friends	8
5 friends	2
4 friends	2
3 friends	1
2 friends	0
1 friends	0
0 friends	0

Because of the results of this research, Arn contends that the friendship ratio is one to seven.[8] He says that each family should make at least seven friends within six months of coming to a church for the first time to ensure that the family will join the church and stay.

While it may seem like a challenge to attract families to a church and another challenge to encourage families to join, in reality, the work is just beginning. Roy M. Oswald and Speed B. Leas, authors of *The Inviting Church: A Study of New Member Assimilation*, say there are six levels of incorporating members into the church. Family members need to not only join but also belong, participate, search, journey inward, and journey outward.[9] In order to move beyond the "joining" stage, Oswald and Leas say, that families need places and groups where they feel they can belong. "After people feel that they have 'gotten in' the church . . . they look for ways to belong," they write. "That is, they want to be known by some of the other members and they want to know other members. They join and become active in groups. These may be classes, choirs, teams, clubs, or prayer groups."[10]

MORE INFO

A Journal on Family Ministry

Published four times a year, *Family Ministry* is a mainline Christian journal that includes articles about family ministry, snapshots of congregations with family ministry programs, book reviews, and research findings. Contact: *Family Ministry,* Louisville Presbyterian Theological Seminary, 1044 Alta Vista Road, Louisville, KY 40205-1798; family@femf.org; http://www.fmef.org.

What Families Tend to Find

While a church may have a lot of activities, the problem is that typical church activities tend to segregate family members from each other. Parents go to committee meetings, adult-only

CHURCH SPOTLIGHT

A Quieting Room

In the 1950s, many churches designed "crying rooms" as a place for families to take their crying and noisy children during worship. Today many churches are removing these rooms so that families don't feel "penalized" and "forced to leave" when their children become too boisterous. At Our Savior Catholic Church in Mobile, Alabama, the church added a "quieting room" that has two entrances: one from the sanctuary and one from the foyer. It provides parents easy access to move into the room during the service or immediately after communion while also making it easy for them to return to the service once the children are ready. Unlike the crying rooms, which were designed for families to spend the rest of the service in, the quieting room is a place for families to go for a short time before returning to the service.

choirs or music groups, adult education, or adult Bible studies. Children go to children's choirs, children's Sunday school classes, and children's activities. Teenagers go to youth groups, youth choirs, and youth-service opportunities. In some churches, children even worship separately from their families or go to a different program halfway through the service. Everybody goes in a different direction.

In smaller churches, especially ones with few families, there may be only a few activities; and these activities may not seem to fit families. The adult education class may be focused more on issues for seniors, especially if the leader and most of those who attend are retired. There may be one Sunday school class for children that includes kindergartners through sixth graders, and the parents are expected to teach or help with the class.

Some churches claim they have intergenerational events for the entire family, such as church picnics, church fix-up times, and church potlucks. Yet if there are few families, the parents often spend most of the time at these events supervising their children (and not connecting with other members of the church). Or parents may feel frustrated because their children don't like the food or are bored because there aren't ways for the children to also participate.

A local church can create a family ministry emphasis that overcomes these difficulties and pitfalls. Churches that succeed in family ministry (by not only attracting families but also keeping them coming for years) are the ones that help families feel that they belong, that they matter, and that they are missed when they are absent. They are the churches that intentionally build ways for family members to grow spiritually not only as individuals but also as a family group. They are the churches that are thinking through the implications for family ministry and are not afraid to ask families for feedback.

> ### MEMORABLE QUOTE
>
> "A church can and should make every effort to help the family be an enriching community for each member." Richard P. Olson and Joe H. Leonard, Jr., *A New Day for Family Ministry*[11]

What Families Have to Say

Many churches make assumptions about families, especially if they have a number of family-friendly mechanisms in place. Many churches assume that families worship together and each family member attends a different education class. In reality, however, that may not be the case. In some cases, the parents may drop off children at church, and the parents never attend a worship service, education class, or anything else. In churches with more than one worship service, parents may attend worship at the same time their children go to the education hour (which means the parents never attend Christian education classes and the children never attend worship). In other churches, parents may be teaching a Sunday school class and may never come to a worship service or any other church activity. Ministry leaders need to discover how families are involved in the congregation and what they're looking for.

Some churches have church leaders who visit each family in their home and ask for their feedback about the church. Others create written surveys. Some form small family groups and provide child care at church, where the groups gather to talk about the strengths and weaknesses of the church. Regardless of the way feedback is gathered, churches must be prepared to hear what families have to say. Families may tell you things about your church that you didn't know about, or they may challenge some of the church's basic philosophies and beliefs.

When families at one family-friendly church were asked for their feedback, church leaders were surprised by the large outcry of parents who felt

MORE INFO

Association of Family Life Professionals

This nonprofit organization brings together church leaders, counselors, psychologists, lawyers, teachers, and any Christian who emphasizes the "basic need for Christ to be the center of all family life." It has a quarterly newsletter, a professional journal, workshops, an annual convention, and a national network of members. For more information, contact Association of Family Life Professionals (AFLP), 3724 Executive Center Drive, Suite 155, Austin, TX 78731; (800) 393-8918.

burned out by the church. The church had always had a philosophy of "It takes a whole village to raise a child" and assigned parents of infants and toddlers each to take turns staffing the church nursery throughout the year. However, parents of infants and toddlers were quick to point out that the church defined "village" as "parents with infants and toddlers" and that many of these parents came to church to be refreshed and renewed only to find that they had nursery duty every six weeks and had to miss worship entirely.

Parents at this church asked if the church truly believed that "it takes a whole village to raise a child," why wasn't every member assigned nursery duty? Or if the church really believed it was family friendly, why didn't it invest money in the nursery and hire regular child-care providers to staff it? One parent related that she was leaving the church because she and her husband were considering having a third child, but the thought of doing all

CHURCH SPOTLIGHT

Ministering to Single Parents

Praise Assembly Church in Crystal, Minnesota, created the "Dream Again Network" for single parents and their children. The ministry includes a weekly, free Saturday program that begins with a 10 A.M. brunch. Afterward, the children attend special events while their parents attend sessions on Christian parenting and Christian financial planning. For single parents with financial difficulties, the ministry also offers "shopping" at the church clothes closet and a free haircut.

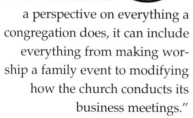

MEMORABLE QUOTE

"Family ministry can take many forms. Because it is a perspective on everything a congregation does, it can include everything from making worship a family event to modifying how the church conducts its business meetings."

Diana R. Garland, *Family Ministry: A Comprehensive Guide*[12]

the assigned nursery duty was weighing on their decision making for their family plan, which they felt was detrimental.

Some leaders were at first taken aback, especially the lay leaders who had created this process twenty years ago when there were fifteen families with young children in the church; but they listened. A child-care provider was hired. Parents with infants and toddlers could now attend worship services every Sunday.

Not only are individual congregations finding out what families have to say, but so are denominations. The ELCA Department for Research and Evaluation found that families with children don't stay for long once they do start attending a church. In a recent study, this denomination discovered that families with children between the ages of 6 and 12 are apt to come to church regularly, but families with children of other ages do not.[13]

The same study also found that divorced or separated people, couples living together, immigrants, people with disabilities, gays and lesbians, people of color, families with young children, families with teenagers and young adults, and empty-nest families aren't likely to come to church. Robert Hoyt of the ELCA's Division for Outreach says these people stay away because their needs aren't being met. "A congregation that is not needs-meeting is not doing the job it was called to do," he says.[14]

What Families Do and Do Not Do

Besides listening to what families say, it's also important to know what families are doing—and not doing—to nurture the spiritual lives of their children at home. "Studies show that large numbers of mainline Christian families no longer read the Bible with their children, pray with them, or talk about faith in daily life," says Roland Martinson, a family ministry expert. The result is that "kids perceive that we do 'God things' at church, and this doesn't have much to do with life."[15]

This lack of integration reflects what family life often is like these days. If families are active in church, those activities are segmented for Sunday and possibly one other day of the week. School and work take up the bulk of the time. There may be music lessons, Boy Scouts or Girl Scouts, sports teams, occasionally family get-togethers, homework, and more. Families live fragmented lives because they have so many pieces to juggle, and few have the time (or the encouragement) to help them put all the pieces together into a puzzle that actually makes sense. That's where the local church has an essential role to play: helping families sort through all the pieces, put them together, and find meaning in the lives they live.

Doing this requires vision, thoughtfulness, and sensitivity to families and the issues with which they're dealing. Although we may have strong biblical and theological opinions about divorce, abortion, living together, homosexuality, and other issues, we need to be sensitive to families in our church who may be dealing with these situations. For example, one fourth-grade boy came home from Sunday school upset because he learned that anyone who was divorced was a sinner. His favorite aunt was divorced. A teenager was confused about her family and what the church was teaching about fornication because her parents had lived together for ten years but weren't married. Another child knew how much she enjoyed being with her friend and her friend's two moms, but after going to Sunday school and learning about the church's view of homosexuality, she wasn't so sure anymore.

What Scripture Says

MORE INFO

A Helpful Family Ministry Book

A New Day for Family Ministry by Richard P. Olson and Joe H. Leonard, Jr., examines the trends of how families are changing and how the church can best welcome different types of families, even when the church has theological difficulties with some of the decisions and issues these families are dealing with. This book is about how to make the church fit for families and how to be sensitive about diverse family issues.

Unfortunately the Bible doesn't have a lot to say about families and family life. What it does say, can often feel judgmental to families today and can drive them away from the church. In John 4, Jesus spoke to the woman at the well who was living with her boyfriend (and had been married five times before that). Because of the way Jesus treated her and spoke to her, the woman felt Jesus cared about her rather than judging or condemning her. The message in John 4 is to welcome people in spite of the choices they've made.

With so many split and fragmented families in our society today, a caring congregation can emphasize how a family can stay together—no matter what configuration the family takes. We can teach about the important qualities that each family member can have (to be loving, to be patient, to be generous, and to be kind, as stated in Galatians 5:22-23) that will strengthen family relationships and create a faith-filled life.

We can show how Jesus used the metaphor of the parent-child relationship as a way to teach about our relationship with God. (See Luke 11:9-13.) For families that are working hard to be family, these scriptures will be meaningful. Yet we also need to be sensitive to families that are dealing with abuse issues who may find these same scripture passages painful and confusing. Child psychologist Ava Siegler cites recent studies that reveal the way children feel about their parents is most likely to determine how they feel about God.[16] How are we helping children with these issues? What about the parents who had difficult family experiences as children? For families in pain, we can bring words of healing and hope, such as in Psalm 23:4 and Isaiah 40:29-31. We can emphasize the importance of pulling together during hard times instead of pulling apart, as Ecclesiastes 4:9-12 suggests.

Many parents will be familiar with corporal punishment in the Bible (such as in Proverbs 13:24 and 23:13-14), yet spanking is now seen by many as abusive. Even the American Academy of Pediatrics "strongly opposes striking a child."[17] It's better instead to stress the importance of loving and guiding a child with the use of discipline instead of punishing a child. Although Proverbs 1:8 and Proverbs 4:1-4 say that children should listen to their parents, Ephesians 6:1-4 says that parents also need to be sensitive to their children.

What Churches Can Do

In parents' struggle to raise their children in the best way, most are isolated and have few resources to rely on. Extended family may live far away—or relationships may be strained. Many parents don't know their neighbors or others in their community. With the rising rates of divorce and single-parent families, often parents are raising children alone and without support. More than ever before, families need the church.

By ministering to families, churches can meet a critical need of helping families find an anchor and a source of strength in a society that seems to have gone adrift. In an endless sea of activities and demands, churches can help families make sense of the currents that pull them in many directions. A church can be a place of calm in the midst of a daily life that sometimes feels like living in a hurricane.

A church doesn't need big budgets, extra staff, or lots of room to minister to families. All a church needs is a vision and a commitment. Families are looking for a place to be renewed and strengthened. They're seeking something that will help them find meaning and purpose. When families become part of your congregation, will they find those things? When families feel welcomed, cared for, and nurtured, they'll want to come and participate fully in the life of your congregation.

Chapter 2

Program Basics

Innovative Ways to Build an Effective Family Ministry

In churches that begin to have an emphasis on family ministry, the typical process is to brainstorm ideas, pick the best ones, and start creating events, workshops, and classes. If an idea works, the church does it again. If an idea flops, the church goes on to something else.

Creating an effective family ministry, however, requires moving from a hodgepodge of ideas to an intentional strategic ministry for families. Planning is key and so is the mentality of moving slowly so that you can make sure the foundation you have poured has time to set and become strong.

This chapter outlines seven key steps to building an effective family ministry. Involve families in these steps so that they have a role in shaping the ministry in a way that meets their needs. Include key church staff and instrumental lay leaders in the process so that they buy into your ministry and will want to get involved by doing their part to make it successful.

Step 1: Understand Families Today

To minister effectively to families, you need to know who families are. In a Search Institute survey of more than two thousand

Family Issues in Scripture

The Bible includes a number of stories about different types of families and the issues they grapple with. Use these in doing Bible studies with families or as discussion starters.

Adoptive Families
Esther was adopted by Mordecai (Esther 2:15, 20)

Biological Families
Ruth and Boaz (Ruth 4:13-22)

Educating Children About Faith
Teach children and explain why faith is important (Deuteronomy 4:9-13; 6:4-9, 20-25)

Family Business
Some businesses have been in families for years (1 Chronicles 4:14, 21-23)

Forgiveness and Parenting
Parable of the Lost Son (Luke 15:11-32)

Grandparents
Jacob blessed his grandsons Ephraim and Manasseh and

(continued on next page)

seventh- to twelfth-graders active in five mainline denominations, researchers found that 79 percent lived with their biological mother and father, 8 percent lived with one parent, 7 percent lived in a blended family, and 5 percent lived in an adoptive family.[1]

This does not reflect the percentage of families nationwide, however. The U.S. Census Bureau found that 68 percent of children eighteen years old and younger live with two parents, which could mean either as an adoptive family, a blended family, or a traditional family. Another 27 percent live in single-parent homes. Four percent live in a family without any parents: a family led by an extended family member (such as a grandparent or aunt or uncle) or in a foster family.[2]

When you look closer at single-parent families, the U.S. Census Bureau reports that 39 percent of single parents are adults who never married. Another 35 percent are divorced. Twenty-two percent are married, but the spouse isn't around; and 4 percent are widowed. Eighty-five percent of single-parent families have only the mother present; 15 percent have only the father.[3]

In a study of sixth- to twelfth-grade young people living in single families, researchers found that young people are more likely to "thrive" (meaning less likely to participate in risky behaviors, such as drinking alcohol, taking drugs, and having premarital sex) when they attend church on a regular basis compared to young people who don't attend church.[4] Churches, as a whole, tend to draw more two-parent families where both parents are the biological parents of all the children in the family. Yet, many families are being overlooked in a community, especially those who don't fit the traditional church norm.

Step 2: Create a Vision and a Mission

It's difficult to reach out to any type of family, however, if you don't know why you want families to connect with your church. That's why it's helpful to name what you want (a vision) and how you

---

Family Issues in Scripture
(continued)

treated them as if they were his sons (Genesis 48:5-16)

Infertility
Sarah and Abraham
(Genesis 17:1-22)
Hannah and Elkanah
(1 Samuel 1:3-20; 2:18-21)
Elizabeth and Zechariah
(Luke 1:5-25)

Interracial Marriages
Ruth of Moab married Boaz of
Israel (Ruth 4:9-10)
Timothy had a Greek father and
a Jewish mother (Acts 16)

Lack of Faith in Parenting
A parent had little faith
(Mark 9:17-29)

Marriage
Physical and spiritual union
(Genesis 2:21-24;
Mark 10:6-9)

Older Adults Starting Families
Sarah and Abraham
(Genesis 21:1-8)
Elizabeth and Zechariah
(Luke 1:57-80)

(continued on next page)

Family Issues in Scripture
(continued)

Sick Children
Jairus and his wife had an ailing
12-year-old daughter
(Mark 5:21-43)

Single-Parent Families
Mother and her sons (1 Kings
17:8-15, 2 Kings 4:1-7)

Transcultural Adoptive Family
Pharaoh's daughter adopted
Moses (Exodus 2:10)

Twins
Twins Esau and Jacob were born
to Rebecca and Isaac
(Genesis 25:19-27)

Two-Career Families
Priscilla and Aquila
(Acts 18:2-3, 18)
Huldah and Shallum
(2 Kings 22:14-20)

Working Woman
Deborah was an Israelite judge
and a prophet (Judges 4:4-5)

Worried Parents
Mary and Joseph lost track of
Jesus (Luke 2:41-52)

generally hope to get there (a mission). A vision is a one- to four-sentence statement that articulates a picture of what a family ministry could look like. It's the big picture, the dream. A mission, on the other hand, is a statement that focuses on how you generally hope to achieve your vision. Mission statements are narrower than vision statements, but they're still rather global in the way they're articulated.

It's important to create a vision statement before the mission statement; however, church leaders often have a hard time with visions because they're viewed as vague. Yet, churches that take the time to go through a visioning process are more likely to have a successful family ministry because they've discussed and struggled with what they're aiming for.

To experience a visioning process, bring together key leaders of your congregation, including paid staff and lay ministry people. Have a brainstorming session in which individuals dream about what a family ministry at your church would look like. Ask the question: "If a visiting family asked our church what we're doing for families that's attracting so much attention, what would we like to say?" Encourage people to dream big, not worry about budgets or personnel—even be a bit outlandish. Write everyone's ideas down on newsprint.

After you finish brainstorming, categorize all the ideas into themes. Have those present vote for their top five statements. Ask everyone to give their first choice five stars, their second choice four stars, their third choice three stars, their fourth choice two stars, and their fifth choice one star. After people finish, add up all the stars and show the ranking. Depending on the outcome, have more discussions, try another vote, or begin work on a vision statement. After you have agreed on a vision statement, give a copy of it to each person and set another meeting one to four weeks later. Give people time to think about the vision statement before you commit to it as a church.

After you have identified a vision statement, go through the same process to create a mission statement. This time, however, ask these questions: "Who? What? How?" In other words, "Who are we ministering to in our family ministry?" "What are we hoping to provide through our family ministry?" "How do we hope to provide these things?" In creating a mission statement, be careful not to get too specific since the statement needs to reflect your family ministry as well as the possible changes you could make in it.

Consider this vision and mission statement:

- *Vision statement:* We at First Church envision a family ministry where all types of families and family members feel welcomed, nurtured, and strengthened as individuals and families of faith.
- *Mission statement:* We hope to contribute to the present and future spiritual well-being of all families through Christian education, worship, congregational care, special programs, and faith-based activities families can do at home.

Another church could come up with a vision and mission statement like this:

- *Vision statement:* We believe that St. Paul's Church is a caring congregation that meets the needs of all families within our community and walks with them as they journey on their spiritual paths, as individuals and as families.
- *Mission statement:* We plan to equip all parents, youth, and children to grow spiritually through worship, service, education, fellowship, and their individual callings. We hope to nurture closer family relationships through programs and activities that also help family members grow deeper in their relationship with Christ.

Notice that the mission statement is more specific than the vision statement, yet it is still broad and somewhat vague. The mission statement for St. Paul's Church names worship, service, education, fellowship, programs, and activities as *how* the church hopes to do family ministry. The church can then work to identify more specifically how families will grow spiritually through all those broad categories by creating ministry plans, but first the church needs to talk about where to position the ministry in relation to other ministries of the church.

Step 3: Make Family Ministry a Major Focus

At this point, it's often tempting to advocate for more staffing (such as hiring a minister of families, youth, and children) and to make family ministry a separate ministry of the church. However, staffing a family ministry may cause it to be viewed as this year's church emphasis (which means it will not receive that same attention next year) or it may become sidelined because it's seen as a specific ministry that focuses on only a certain segment of the church. In some churches, family ministry gets attached to the youth ministry. When this happens, the family ministry gradually becomes focused on families with teenagers instead of all families in the church. The family ministry loses credibility in the church at large because it is considered an offspring of youth ministry, a ministry overlooked by many adults in the church because of the uncomfortable feelings many people may have with teenagers.

FAST FACT

How families in Mainline Denominations compare

Families look slightly different according to the denomination they belong to:

	CC (DOC)	ELCA	PCUSA	UCC	UMC
2-parent biological families	72%	78%	75%	78%	81%
Single-parent families	14%	9%	12%	8%	6%
Blended families	8%	7%	10%	8%	6%
Adoptive families	5%	5%	3%	7%	5%

CC (DOC) is the Christian Church (Disciples of Christ); ELCA is the Evangelical Lutheran Church in America; PCUSA is the Presbyterian Church (U.S.A.), UCC is the United Church of Christ, and UMC is The United Methodist Church.[5]

CHURCH SPOTLIGHT

Dynamite Dads

Leon Castle of First Baptist Church in Charlottesville, Virginia, believes that more men should get involved in children's church education. "It communicates that spiritual things are important, that godliness is manly," he says. At Shannon Baptist Church in Columbia, South Carolina, a husband and wife teach mission classes together so that children get the influence of both a man and a woman. Plus, by teaching together, the couple have grown closer in ways they couldn't imagine.[6]

Therefore, it's best to keep family ministry as a central role of the church. All paid staff as well as all committees should have an active role in family ministry. In fact, it may be helpful to name the broad categories for your church membership: such as *families, singles,* and *older adults*. (Your church may end up with more categories than three.) Examine these broad categories whenever you make any decision in a committee. Analyze each new (and old) ministry program and activity with these categories in mind so that you can ensure that there's an aspect of the ministry that addresses the needs of each group. Only then can the congregation be more intentional about welcoming all types of people and families who come through the doors. Only then can the church meet more of the needs of the wide variety of its membership.

Step 4: Examine Your Current Programs

After you've created a vision statement and a mission statement, and decided where to position your family ministry in the context of all your church ministries, it's time to begin identifying the specific ways families can be involved in your church. Some people call these ministry plans. Others call them ministry programs. Still others say they're ministry activities. Whatever name you use, they're the specific ways you'll reach your mission and vision for family ministry in your church.

It's tempting to start jumping in and developing new programs, new ministries, and new activities when you're starting a family ministry. You'll be more successful (and less likely to burn out and have the family ministry crash and burn) if you first look at what your church already offers. Examine each ministry, program, and activity to see how it could integrate families and meet their needs.

• **Christian education**—All churches have some sort of Christian education system already in place. Examine your children's education, youth education, and adult education. Is the topic of family life ever studied? How are parents being educated in your church? How are families receiving education together? See chapter 3 for ideas about how to integrate family ministry into your current Christian education classes.

• **Service and mission**—Most churches have service and mission projects, even if they only do one annual project a year (such as cleaning up the side of a highway, having a church fix-up day, or partnering with another organization, such as Habitat for Humanity). How can families become involved in service and mission projects? Chapter 4 outlines ideas and issues to consider as you begin.

MEMORABLE QUOTE

"Family ministry is not just a set of programs that address family issues. . . . Family ministry includes everything a church and its representatives do."

Diana R. Garland,
Family Ministry:
A Comprehensive Guide, p. 374.

MORE INFO

A Helpful Family Ministry Resource

Passing On the Faith, by Merton P. Strommen and Richard A. Hardel presents a new model for youth and family ministry. Not only does it address how to reach and keep families but it also emphasizes the importance of the ministry churches provide for young people.[7]

• **Worship**—How to integrate families in worship is a hot debate in many churches. Some churches have a separate children's worship. Others have a contemporary service that's more focused on families. Still others are intentional about including families in traditional worship services. Whatever method you choose, it is essential that your church includes families in worship. You'll find ideas for making worship services more family friendly in chapter 5.

• **Congregational care**—Churches typically think of pastoral care as caring for the sick, the hospitalized, and the homebound. Yet families also need care. What about the family going through a divorce? What about a family worried about a child having out-patient surgery? When you expand the area of pastoral care, it becomes clear that a pastor or your pastoral staff will quickly become overwhelmed. It's helpful to consider how all members of the congregation can play a role in this essential ministry of the church by renaming it congregational care. See chapter 6 for ideas about how to create congregational care for families.

• **Music and the arts**—Many families have children who take music lessons, and a number of families enjoy making music

together. How can your church make its music ministry more inclusive for families? How can families be more involved in worship through music and the arts? Chapter 7 gives a number of ideas.

• **Special activities**—Your church may have fellowship activities, sport activities, camps, and retreats. How can families become involved in these activities? What other special activities could you add that would attract families? You'll find a number of special activities for families in chapter 8.

• **Take-home activities**—For children and youth to be raised in the Christian faith, families need to integrate faith in their daily lives at home. The church has an important role here, yet it's a role that's often overlooked since the results are more long term than short term. It's easier to invest energy in a parent workshop on Sunday morning because you can immediately tell that ten parents attended. If you send home a family devotional, you often do not know if any family used it. Chapter 9 outlines a number of ways for churches to encourage families to build faith at home on a daily basis.

• **Other areas of your church**—Your church may have other ministry areas where you should include families in some way. Even the properties or church facilities committee can benefit from families, if you are creative. For example, maybe the properties committee has identified that it will start a church library, and shelves are needed. How about making this a service project for families who enjoy carpentry?

Think about church committees in general. How many parents are members? What are the time commitments you require

CHURCH SPOTLIGHT

Reaching out to families

Sixty Detroit churches have come together to help three hundred families move from welfare to work. Together the churches created a program called Project GAP (God Always Provides). Mentors within each church help build the work skills of individual families. "Students bond, become friends, phone each other," says Edna Scott, the director of the project. "Most start attending church where they take class. We promise, 'For every step you take, we'll take three or four.'" Each church involved in the project commits to helping each family for one year—even if the family gets back on its feet sooner than that.[8]

for a committee member? For example, one church council found that no parent in the congregation would commit to a three-year term on the church council because parents had heard that council meetings often ran for five to six hours (past midnight), and they felt they would miss some critical stages of their children's lives. (Remember that for a parent of a three-year-old, a three-year term includes the child's entire preschool years and the beginning of kindergarten. If the parent has a sixteen-year-old, the child will graduate before the three-year term is up.) What about rethinking your church committees? What about occasionally inviting parents to come to give the committee feedback and suggestions? Or what about mandating that two committee members must be parents and that you'll create four-month terms for parents so terms are shorter and more manageable?

Step 5: Set Your Family Ministry Agenda

Once you know what your church offers, begin to create your family ministry agenda by enhancing the programs, activities, and ministries that already exist so that they're family friendly. If you find holes, begin to create some new activities—but start slow. It's more productive to create two or three new activities than to create a brand new family ministry. That way you can try the few activities you've set up, to see how well they're attended, and also get feedback.

> ## MEMORABLE QUOTE
>
> "Neither the single-parent family nor the nuclear family can bear alone the responsibility of Christian nurture. We need an extended family, the Church, to help us be faithful with our children and to support us in the nurturing of our children in the Christian faith."
>
> John H. Westerhoff III, *Bringing Up Children in the Christian Faith*[9]

Feedback is essential. Not only do you want to hear from the families who attended but you especially need to find out why families didn't attend. For example, in some communities families find themselves having to choose between an organized sport game and a church activity—or even worship. In Boston, a group of congregations worked with the city's parks and recreation department to help raise money for outdoor lighting to free fields in the evenings so families wouldn't have to choose between worship on Sunday mornings and a game. These churches would have never learned about these conflicts if they hadn't asked families why they weren't coming to church activities. Neither would these churches have come together to work with the city's parks and recreation if they hadn't started talking to each other and discovered that every church was experiencing the same difficulty and frustration.

Feedback also gives you information about how well you're reaching your vision, mission, and goals. For example, a survey of five hundred religious youth workers found that 45 percent say that supporting and educating parents is a very important goal of their ministry, yet only 6 percent say they do this very well.[10]

When you compare faith traditions, you find that evangelical and Catholic churches are more likely to have a goal of supporting and educating parents than mainline churches. While 53 percent of evangelical and 48 percent of Catholic religious youth workers say that it's very important for them to support and educate parents, only 38 percent of mainline religious youth workers agree.[11]

In another study, 52 percent of adults say "the congregation intentionally strengthens family life," while 44 percent of young people in these families believe this is true. When asked if the congregation helps parents learn how to nurture the faith of their children, only 20 percent of parents said yes.[12] Getting feedback as you set your family ministry agenda will help you better meet the needs of families as you tweak programs, change directions, or scrap one activity for another.

Step 6: Continue to Learn

As you create a family ministry and watch it evolve, continue to seek out resources and new ideas to keep families engaged and your church up-to-date on the latest family ministry trends. Throughout this book, you'll find other family ministry resources in the "More Info" sidebar boxes of each chapter. You'll also find "Fast Facts," "Memorable Quotes," and "Church Spotlights" in each chapter, which give you more information to consider. In chapters 3 through 9, you'll discover bul-

---

MORE INFO

A

Comprehensive

Resource

Family Ministry: A Comprehensive Guide by Diana R. Garland is the most comprehensive guide on family ministry available. Within the 627-page book (which is an ideal textbook for seminaries and universities), you'll find helpful information on the characteristics of strong families, an in-depth section of biblical foundations for family ministry, and ideas about how to plan and lead a family ministry.

leted ideas on how to include family ministry within a particular ministry in the church along with a "Bonus Idea."

Get on the mailing lists of denominational publishing houses so that you can see what your denomination and other denominations are offering in the area of family ministry. Find out if your denomination has a family ministry division (or a family ministry subdivision of another division). Use the comprehensive family ministry notebook: *Family Works: A Publication of the Center for Ministry Development*, which includes family enrichment activities, parenting workshops, family learning activities, family rituals and celebrations, and family service activities.[13] Look at *Building Assets in Congregations*, a book that presents a research model of forty key factors (called assets) that children and youth need to succeed. Chapter 6 of that book focuses on family ministry.[14]

Once you become more established with your family ministry, connect with other churches in your denomination or community who are also doing family ministry. Meet together once a month and talk about the ups and downs of reaching out and working with families. If you attend an annual denominational convention, try to create a gathering of people who are doing family ministry and start your own network. Find out what's working in other churches. Ask about which pitfalls to avoid.

Step 7: Keep Going

Doing family ministry will raise all kinds of issues that won't be easy to solve. How do you keep families together when one family member practices a different faith tradition—or isn't religious at all? How do you nurture faith in families when one family can literally change from week to week, depending on who has custody of the children and how many different parents are involved? How do you reach out to families in your community who speak a different language than you do—or who grew up in a different culture with a different set of values?

Along the way, you'll encounter obstacles, high walls, potholes, politics, personalities (the ones that like to get in your way), and other difficulties that may try to pull you off course. You may even consider quitting. Don't. As Mother Teresa said, "God hasn't called me to be successful. [God's] called me to be faithful."[15]

Family ministry veterans know it takes a long time for a family ministry to take root. In planting seeds, some will sprout. Others will not. What's essential is to keep planting, keep watering, keep fertilizing, and keep an eye on the conditions around you. Some years will be stormy. Others will be more quiet and calm. Some years you'll wonder if anything will grow at all. Other years, you'll enjoy a bumper crop.

Take time to start slowly and build with intention. Tap into what's working at your church. Throw out what's not. Be faithful in what you've been called to do. Keep going—no matter what.

Chapter 3

Exciting Education

Meeting Needs Through Learning

Most churches are well versed in the traditions of Christian education: Create classrooms of same-age children and have a class (or possibly two) for adults. People seem to learn by being with their peers and using a curriculum that's geared for their age group.

A number of churches, however, are trying something new: *intergenerational* and *family* educational opportunities. They're rethinking how children, teenagers, and adults learn and questioning whether keeping these groups separate is really the best way to educate families.

While intergenerational and family educational classes are ideal ways to bring family members closer and to introduce people to others of different ages in the church, these types of classes can be challenging to implement. They take much more planning than traditional education classes because finding learning activities that benefit people of different age groups isn't easy. In addition, many members don't understand intergenerational learning and end up not attending.

FAST FACT

Busy Schedules

The two most common problems confronting Christian educators in Protestant churches is adults' busy schedules (say 72 percent of coordinators) and young people's busy schedules (say 66 percent of coordinators).[1]

MORE INFO

Family Sunday School Curriculum

Total Family Sunday School (TFSS) is an intergenerational small group educational system that helps children, youth, and parents learn from each other, pray for each other, and create projects. It is developed by Rev. Richard Melheim, executive director of the Faith Inkubators Project, a Christian education systems think tank. Available from Faith Inkubators Project, (888)-55FAITH; info@faithink.com; http:www.tfss.com.

"Intergenerational Christian education is vital to the ministry of the church because younger persons need to hear and learn from older persons (Deuteronomy 6:6-7), and older persons need to hear and learn from younger persons (Isaiah 11:6)," writes Diana Garland, editor of the journal *Family Ministry: Empowering Through Faith.*[2] Unfortunately, many families are used to being age segregated through their experiences with schools, work, extended family, community, and extracurricular activities. Many just don't have the experience of the benefits of knowing and learning from people of different generations.

Churches often use the term *intergenerational* to mean family education, yet there is a distinct difference between inter-generational education and family education. Intergenerational education focuses on bringing people of all ages in the church together, from infants through the eldest member. In doing so, family members may be put into different small groups so that individuals can get to know more people. The overall goal of intergenerational education is to get more people within the church to interact with other people they typically wouldn't come into contact with and to learn together side by side.

Family education, in contrast, has the goal of keeping family members together and getting the entire family engaged in a specific Christian education topic. Often subjects are about family issues, such as family communication and family religious rituals. The underlying mission of family education is to bring family members together and to strengthen relationships between family members through education.

Besides bringing people together, intergenerational and family education classes can also interject more life into your Christian education program throughout the year. When does your church experience the largest numbers in Christian education classes? For most churches, this is around rally or welcome-back Sunday, the Sunday following Labor Day. Attendance tends to be strong for a month or two and then typically the numbers begin to dwindle through the rest of the year with occasional increases around Advent and Easter. Some churches see strong links between the weather and attendance, or the seasons and attendance. Experiment with the timing of intergenerational and family classes during low-ebb and high-ebb times to determine what works best in your church.

Some churches create two educational tracks: one for the same-age educational classes and one for intergenerational and family classes. Larger churches may have these tracks going on simultaneously while smaller churches may schedule three Sundays each month for same-age educational classes and one Sunday a month for an intergenerational and/or a family class. Different people are recruited to lead these two tracks so that fewer adults experience burnout as Christian education teachers and so that teachers can have an occasional much-needed break.

Other churches start more slowly in the area of family ministry education and begin by offering parent education classes so that parents' needs and concerns are addressed. A church can offer these classes during the education hour on Sunday or as an evening class during the week. Some congregations provide child care to make it easier for parents to attend. Other churches begin even more simply by asking each children's Sunday school class to schedule one class during the year that will be for both parents and children.

The important considerations in making decisions about your Christian education program regarding family ministry are your goals:

- *Who do you wish to bring together?*

- *What do you hope to accomplish?*

- *What learning strategies do you have for your family ministry?*

Thinking through your ministry goals will help you be more intentional in setting up classes and programs that are effective. Getting people's feedback along the way will also ensure that you stay on track.

Family Education Ideas

- ***Create parent-child book groups.*** Have parents and children read the same book, then come together to discuss the book. Families with upper elementary-age children (fourth- through sixth-graders) could read *Number the Stars* by Lois Lowry (Boston: Houghton Mifflin, 1989) about a ten-year-old who helps Jewish friends escape from the Nazis during the German occupation of Denmark, or *Are You There God? It's Me, Margaret* by Judy Blume (New York: Bantam Doubleday Dell, 1970), a book that introduces girls not only to the changes in puberty but also to the struggles of faith. Families with teenage children could read *It's Our World, Too!: Stories of Young People Who Are Making a Difference* by Phillip Hoose (Boston: Little, Brown, & Company, 1993), which profiles inspiring young people who help the environment or take a stand for a better a world, or *To Kill a Mockingbird* by Harper Lee (New York: Warner Books, 1960) the Pulitzer-prize-winning novel about a father who morally educates his children about what's right. There may also be another book that group members suggest.

• *In the summer, have families bring beach towels and blankets to your church.* Have everyone lie outside in the dark to gaze at the stars in the sky. Find constellations. Count stars. Watch for airplanes flying overhead. Talk about God's creation.

• *Have a class on the importance of voting and why being faithful involves being involved in the political process.* (Ensure that the person leading this class is open to discussing how people's faith can lead them to be Republican, Democrat, Reform, or in favor of some other party.) During an election year, have a mock ballot where children, youth, and parents can vote for a candidate to teach the importance of getting involved—even before voting age.

• *Create a class to teach children and parents how to communication with one another more effectively.* In a study of 2,356 Protestant young people, researchers asked participants about twelve different subjects to see which ones the church does a good or excellent job of

CHURCH SPOTLIGHT

Marriage and Family Programs

First United Methodist Church in Shreveport, Louisiana, offers a monthly Marriage Matters class for parents. While couples learn helpful exercises, connect with other couples, and have fun, infants, toddlers, and preschoolers can go to child care and children in elementary school can participate in the First Kids Club.

MEMORABLE QUOTE

"Family ministry means translating biblical concepts of human relationships into practical patterns for family living."

Joe Leonard, Jr.,
Planning Family Ministry[4]

teaching. Learning how to talk with my parents ranked eleventh out of twelve. Only 31 percent of young people say the church does an adequate job of teaching them these skills.[3]

• *If your church has a library, offer family story times* when parents can bring their children and hear Christian children's books read aloud to them.

• *Rent a video or go see a movie* that is appropriate for older children, youth, and parents and discuss the positive and negative values portrayed. Talk about how characters acted on their faith (or didn't act according to religious values) and what viewers learned from the movie.

• *Encourage family members to talk about their faith experiences with one another* by using the game "FaithTalk with Children" from the Youth & Family Institute of Augsburg College, Campus Box 70, 2211 Riverside Avenue, Minneapolis, MN 55454; (877) 239-2492; yfi@augsburg.edu; http://youthfamilyinstitute.com.

Intergenerational Education Ideas

• *Have an intergenerational class where children, youth, and adults come together to learn about the Bible and Christian heroes.* Form small groups (with mixed ages) where people can talk about their faith heroes (in the Bible and in the world).

• *Find people of different ages who would be willing to share some of the significant events that have occurred on*

their faith journeys. Ideally gather two children, two teenagers, one young adult, one younger middle-age adult (in the thirties or forties), one older middle-age adult (in the fifties or early sixties), and one older adult to talk for about five minutes. Offer an inter-generational class featuring these people.

• *Create an intergenerational class on the ethnic heritage of church members' ancestors.* Invite children, youth, and adults to form groups according to their ancestors' state, tribe, or country of origin. Have groups study and talk about the faith of their ancestors and/or the religious issues that were occurring in their native back-ground.

• *Create an intergenerational class that encourages people of different ages to mingle and talk to each other.* For example, give each person a sheet of paper. Have them talk to one child, one teenager, and one adult to find out the person's favorite Bible story and why. Ask them to repeat the activity with three new people to learn their favorite Bible verse and why. Consider other topics such as: favorite Sunday school teacher, favorite religious holiday, favorite religious ritual, and so on.

• *Partner adults with teenagers and children who share the same interests.* For example, adults who enjoy computers can get to know children and teenagers who share that interest. Or adults who enjoy plants can get to know young people who also like to garden. Encourage them to meet to learn from one another and get to know one another.

• *Invite people (from fourth grade and up) to an intergenera-tional class on faith and current events.* Use the current, eight-page issue of *Time for Kids* (which is available for educational purposes by calling 1-800-777-8600) since the short articles are ideal for young people to comprehend and also easy for adults to read quickly. Teach and discuss current events and various Christian responses.

• *Create an intergenerational class that highlights the strengths of children's education and adult education.* For example, adult education tends to do well in terms of dealing with a topic in-depth and creating stimulating discussions. Children's education tends to excel at creating a variety of activities around a topic, such as having a craft, a song, a game, and other activities. Choose a topic that would be of interest to people of different ages (such as deepening your faith) and create a class that has in-depth study, discussion, craft, game, and song.

• *Develop intergenerational educational outings,* such as touring cathedrals and other churches in your area or visiting a Jewish temple to learn the similarities and differences of other denominations and faiths.

• *Create an intergenerational in-depth Bible study of a popular Bible story*, such as the Creation (Genesis 1–2), David and Jonathan (1 Samuel 20, 24), Zacchaeus (Luke 19), or Paul's conversion (Acts 9). Have people use Bible dictionaries, Bible atlases, and other Bible reference books to learn more about the context of the passage.

Parent Educational Ideas

• First-time parents often don't know much about how to interact and play with their young children. *Have classes that teach parents about the developmental issues of children.* For example, have a one-hour parents class to teach parents how to care and play with infants (while the infants are in a nursery) and then bring the infants and parents together for thirty minutes to try different play activities. This also works with other age groups, such as parents and toddlers or parents and preschoolers.

- *Survey the parents of your congregation to learn what topics they're most interested in.* Topics could include discipline, sibling rivalry, picky eaters, extended family issues, too many activities, family faith activities, and so on.

- *Offer classes on basic Christian skills that parents can use at home.* For example, have classes on how to do family prayer, devotions, meditation, and Bible study.

- One area of major conflict for many families is money. *Create parent-education classes on financial management for families.* Include a course on stewardship (based on Scripture) that also teaches the skills for families to contribute financially to the causes they believe in.

- *Provide a class on teaching Christian values to children and youth.* Help parents identify essential values of the Christian faith and how to teach them to their children.

- *Create a short series of parenting classes (possibly three to four classes) on evaluating parents' faith experiences* when they were children and their faith hopes as parents for their children. Give parents time to articulate how their parents nurtured (or didn't nurture) their faith and how they are raising their children in similar and different ways.

- *Develop a class that focuses on a specific type of parenting, such as single parenting, blended-family parenting, two-parent family parenting, and so on.* Ideally have three classes, one on each of these three types of parenting. Not only can you better

CHURCH SPOTLIGHT

Intergenerational VBS

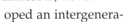

Bethel Lutheran Church in Northfield, Minnesota, developed an intergenerational Bible summer school where adults learn with children and youth. The program emphasized not only learning but also relationship building between children, youth, and adults.

MORE INFO

Marriage Education

The University of Minnesota has created two couple inventories for churches to use: the *Prepare Inventory* (for engaged couples who are going to marry) and the *Enrich Inventory* (for couples who already are married). The inventories help couples talk about issues such as expectations, religious issues, sexuality, children and parenting, conflict resolution, communication, and roles. Contact: Prepare/Enrich Training, Attention: David Olson, P.O. Box 190, Minneapolis, MN 55440; 800-331-1661.

address the specific issues that each type of family has, but you'll also help parents connect with other parents in similar situations.

• *Sponsor an enrichment workshop for parents*. Teach parents skills of caring for themselves when parenting and life demands seem overwhelming. Tie in soothing scripture, such as Psalm 23, Matthew 11:28, and Galatians 6:9. Lead parents in a calming meditation.

• *Offer a class or an ongoing support group for two-parent families that focuses on marriage*. Consider offering a class during the adult education hour at your church while children are in Sunday school or at another time when childcare is available.

• *Teach parents about the importance of family rituals.* Have parents talk about their family rituals, and expose them to new family rituals as well. A helpful resource is *Family Rituals and Celebrations* (written from a Catholic perspective) from the Center for Ministry Development, P.O. Box 699, Naugatuck, CT 06770; (203) 723-1622; http://www.cmdnet.org; E-mail: cmdnet@mindspring.com.

• *Offer classes for parents of children in specific age groups*, such as infants, toddlers, preschoolers, elementary-age children, middle-school teenagers, high-school teenagers, and young adults. (Or consider creating a series called Parenting Through the Life Cycle that focuses on specific issues related to parenting a particular age group.) Help parents connect with other parents who have children the same age.

• *Have a parenting self-reflection class where parents assess their feelings about being a parent.* The confidence levels of parents go up and down depending on the struggles or ease they're having with their children. As a class, examine these issues in light of parental self-esteem.

• *Invite a family therapist, a child development expert, or a parent educator in your community (who also is a Christian) to lead a class on parenting.* Sometimes members of the congregation may be in one of these fields.

• *Develop a five-series parenting class based on the book* **Five Cries of Parents** by Merton P. and A. Irene Strommen (San Francisco: Harper & Row, 1985). The book is based in a Christian theology. Have a class on each one of the five cries: *understanding, close family, moral behavior, shared faith,* and *outside help.*

• *Have a parenting class on a hot topic*, such as talking to your child about sexuality or drug and alcohol use prevention.

Children and Youth Educational Ideas

• *During a Sunday school class or youth group meeting, focus on the topic of family negotiation.* Teach kids the skills of asking for what they want, advocating for themselves, listening, respecting their parents, and managing their emotions.

• *Develop a class where young people assess the relationships they have with each of their family members.* Talk about what makes relationships weak and strong and how to build better relationships with parents and siblings.

• *Have a class to discuss what to do when there's trouble within a family.* Who should children and youth turn to? What resources are available in the church? What if a family member has asked a child to keep a secret that's harmful to the child? Although this is a difficult issue to discuss, it's essential to teach children and youth who they can trust and count on outside of the family.

• *Focus a class on household chores.* Take a survey of young people to see which chores they typically do (such as making their bed, washing dishes, emptying the dishwasher, taking out the garbage, and so on). Talk about the importance of each family member doing household chores and why.

Afterward, compile the class survey and give the results to each parent. This helps parents see how their expectations compare to other parents' expectations in your church.

• *Develop a class about young people's views of marriage and family.* What do young people hope for in their personal future? Why? How do these views tie in to their current experience in their families? What are they learning about families and marriage from their parents?

• *Talk about friendships in regard to how family members accept or don't accept these relationships.* Have a Bible study about friendship, focusing on the positive relationship between David and Jonathan (1 Samuel 18:1-4, 19:1, 20:17 and 2 Samuel 1:26) and the unhelpful relationships of Job's three friends (Job 6:14-15, 12:4, 19:14-24). Talk about the purpose of friendships by examining Deuteronomy 13:6, Proverbs 17:17, Proverbs 18:24, and John 15:12-13.

• *Create a family wish list class.* Have young people articulate what they would like from their families and their parents. Discuss those expectations and how to approach parents about their hopes.

• *Have a "best" class.* Ask young people to either draw pictures or write short essays about what they like best about their families. Have young children (who aren't old enough to write) draw pictures of their families. Display these pictures and essays around your church. During class emphasize the positive aspects of families. Close with a prayer of thanksgiving.

•*Periodically create art projects and crafts during class that would make good mementos for parents to keep.* With young children, use their painted handprints and footprints in crafts. Have older children and youth write letters or poems to their parents. Or create projects that include a child's photograph. Be intentional about doing projects for both mothers and fathers. Since Mother's Day falls during the Sunday school church year (in May) and Father's Day does not (in June), most church-going children make projects only for Mom, not for Dad.

• *Offer a class on money management.* Talk about how young people get their money (through allowances, doing odd jobs around the house, and working) and what their views are about money. Discuss why families have conflicts about money. Tie in scripture related to money, such as Genesis 13:2, Proverbs 28:20, Amos 6:1-2, Matthew 27:57, Luke 8:3, and James 5:1-5. Encourage children and youth to become regular givers of money to the church and to other organizations they believe in.

BONUS IDEA

Bring out the Tribes

Have an intergenerational in-depth study of the twelve tribes of Israel. Assign children, youth, and adults to be members of one of the twelve tribes: Reuben, Simeon, Levi, Judah, Issachar, Zebulun, Joseph, Benjamin, Gad, Asher, Dan, and Naphtali. Transform the class into biblical times and have people experience what it would be like to be a member of one of those tribes through dressing in costume, eating appropriate food, doing crafts, and participating in other activities.

• *Create a class about discussing faith.* Talk about faith during class and find out how often young people talk about faith issues with family members (also include grandparents, aunts, uncles, and cousins). Discuss why faith is often a difficult topic to talk about. Give young people ideas about how to talk to their parents and siblings about faith issues.

•*Include one to two easy, new ideas based on your class topic that young people can take home to do with their families.* Tie in take-home activities when you're studying prayer, meditation, devotions, service, and other faith disciplines.

• *Watch videos that emphasize family values and then discuss them.* For preschoolers, use *VeggieTales.* For elementary-age children, use *Adventures from the Book of Virtues.* For teenagers, use current movies (rated PG or PG-13), such as *October Sky* (released 1999, rated PG) or *Ellen Foster* (released 1997 as a Hallmark Hall of Fame TV movie, rated PG-13). The web site: http://www.imdb.com lists movies and videos along with plot lines and ratings to help you choose.

• *Develop a "What Parents Do" class.* Have young people list all the different activities their parents do in the course of a week. Create other activities that help children and youth become more acquainted and empathetic to the many roles their parents have.

• *Have a family fun class where young people identify the different ways they have fun with their families.* Study the different ways families in the Bible had fun, such as taking trips (Genesis 46:1-15), making music (Exodus 15), visiting friends and family (Luke 1:39-45), and going to church together (Luke 2:41-52).

One-Time Educational Ideas

• *Have an auto mechanic give a short course on car maintenance,* showing parents and young people how to change the oil, how to add other fluids to the car, and what warning signs to watch for. Single parents often appreciate this and so do young people who are interested in cars.

• *Team up with a health organization or medical clinic to teach infant and child CPR to parents at your church.* Publicize the class and invite residents of your community.

• *Ask a hair stylist to lead a class on hair care.* If you have a number of families who cut their children's hair to save money, have the hair stylist give tips to parents on how to do this well.

• *If your church has a kitchen, offer a cooking class for families.* For example, boil eggs at Easter time and have families decorate them or bake unusual holiday cookies during Advent. During other times of the year, offer classes on cooking easy, nutritious meals that children will eat.

• *Offer a class on video equipment.* Although many families own VCRs and camcorders, a number of families struggle with how to use this equipment well. Ask your community cable channel to provide someone who can teach families video basics, along with editing and photograph-to-video transfer techniques. Once a number of families are adept at using camcorders and other video equipment, ask them to videotape worship services or special church events.

• *Have a sleep class for exhausted parents one evening.* Arrange for someone to read stories to the children who come in pajamas and slippers while parents hear an expert give tips on developing consistent bedtime routines and helping children sleep through the night.

• Ask a minister, seminary student, or layperson who knows about young adult books with Christian themes to *give a one-time workshop on choosing Christian books for children and teenagers.*

• For families who also are providing caregiving for aging parents, *offer a sandwich-generation class led by a pastoral care minister or a social services expert on the topic.* Provide sandwiches or sandwich cookies for food.

• *Offer a baby-sitting safety class for older children and teenagers.* Contact the American Red Cross for teachers. After young people have learned baby-sitting skills, create a list of young people who want to baby-sit for other church families. Distribute this list to parents of young children and to families when they join your church.

• *Recruit a Web expert to teach families in your church how to set up a family Web site.* Invite residents of your community to the class through your local newspaper.

• Ask a minister or certified vocational rehabilitation counselor to *lead a workshop on helping family members find their life purpose.*

• *As the new year approaches, offer a class on setting New Year's resolutions.* Encourage individuals to set personal faith resolutions. Teach family members how to stick with resolutions and what to do when they experience setbacks.

• *Invite a nutritionist or therapist who specializes in children's eating habits to offer a class.* Teach parents how to make meal times less stressful. Give parents ideas about how to encourage young people to try new foods, to develop healthy eating habits in their children, and to handle picky eaters.

• *Have a minister lead a class on helping family members identify their spiritual gifts.*

• *Identify a church member who is fluent in a second language to teach a beginning language class.* This is an ideal way for parents and young people to learn a language together.

Chapter 4

Service and Mission

families Help others Together

Family service is one of three critical factors researchers have found that help children and youth grow deeper in faith.[1] Yet 66 percent of children age five to twelve and 63 percent of teenagers age thirteen and older never or rarely do family service projects.[2] More families, however, are looking for service projects to do together and looking to the church to help them identify ways to help others. The challenge is that few churches have experience in creating service projects where all members of a family can participate together.

Researchers have found that there are strong connections between young people getting involved in service and modeling their parents' service involvement. For example, 66 percent of young people who strongly agree that their parents "spend a lot of time helping other people" also say they do at least one hour of volunteer work in an average week. In comparison, of the young people who strongly disagree that their parents spend a lot of time helping other people, only 32 percent of these young people do any volunteer work.[3]

Although the research highlights the importance of family service, many families also see the benefits. Congregations start-

FAST FACT

Common
Family Service
Projects

Family Matters, a project of The Points of Light Foundation, discovered that the top five most common types of volunteer activities for families are: working with children or youth, recreational programs, working with the elderly, sports programs, environmental projects.[4]

ing family service projects are finding that families really want to be involved, but they don't know how and feel uncomfortable doing service projects by themselves without guidance. That's what the service and justice coordinator for the Center for Ministry Development in Naugatuck, Connecticut, discovered when he started designing family service projects at his church in Middlebury, Connecticut. When he began offering family service projects, he was surprised by how many families came. Interest was extremely high.

With the fast-paced life that many families lead, more and more families are looking for activities that bring family members together rather than send them off in different directions. A new group, called Family Life 1st, urges families "to make family time and family activities a high priority in their decision making," to "set conscious limits on the scheduling of outside activities in order to honor the values they hold about family time," to "set limits on electronic media," and to "seek out ways to participate together in activities that build and serve their communities."[5] These four commitments ring true to families who are looking for meaningful activities that bring family members together. Emphasis on family service fulfills these four commitments.

In addition, families who do family service projects find that these experiences challenge individual family members in ways that help them grow. "Family volunteering helps develop . . . stronger bonds by allowing family members to see each other in new roles and gain new appreciation for each other," says Virginia T. Austin of The Points of Light Foundation, an organization that promotes volunteerism. "Volunteering as a family gives young people the opportunity to lead and direct."[6] For one family of Bellevue, Washington, service is a way of life. The family of four frequently does all kinds of service projects. The daughter recently organized a thirty-hour fast to benefit hungry people, after hearing an advertisement for World Vision. She got ten classmates to participate with her and collected $250 in pledges. Although she was the only family member who did this particular service project, her interest in developing a project grew out of her family's commitment to service and a number of family experiences of doing service projects together.

By serving together, families also talk and teach about values. Twelve- to seventeen-year-olds who volunteer say that service projects teach them to respect others, to be helpful and kind, to get along with and relate to others, and to understand people who are different from them.[7] Service projects easily open up a whole range of discussion topics, such as, peace and justice issues, equality, and the value of giving and serving.

MORE INFO

Two Helpful Resources

Beyond Leaf Raking: Learning to Serve/Serving to Learn by Peter L. Benson and Eugene C. Roehlkepartain (Nashville: Abingdon Press, 1993) is a comprehensive guide for engaging teenagers in service. *Teaching Kids to Care & Share* by Jolene L. Roehlkepartain (Nashville: Abingdon Press, 2000) gives more than three hundred mission and service project ideas for children aged three to twelve.

While a significant amount of research has been conducted on adults doing service, very little is available on family service.[8] However, researchers are beginning to examine the impact of service on children and youth. The Independent Sector in Washington, D.C., periodically releases an updated study on the giving and serving patterns of volunteers, and the organization includes specific information about young people.

What makes service projects empowering for children and youth? Researchers have found that it is essential that young people:

- do the actual work and don't just observe,

- work with accepting adults who don't criticize their efforts,

- have important responsibilities,

- have a sense that they can make a contribution,

- have the freedom to explore their own interests and develop their own ideas,

- have opportunities to reflect about the meaning of the activity.[9]

Easy Ideas to Get Started

- *Be clear about expectations and roles.* It's important for each family member to do actual work and not just observe. Too often it's easy to engage the adults and leave out the youngest children. Another challenge is to make sure parents aren't the leaders and children the followers. Rotate the leadership of activities within a service project so that each family member gets a chance to lead.

• *Develop a cooperative atmosphere.* People who volunteer want to work with accepting adults who don't criticize their efforts. This is true of adults, teenagers, and children.

• *Train families.* This ties into the component of giving participants important responsibility. Many families don't know how to volunteer together as a family (and many churches don't either). Only three of five young people in churches say they have spent at least six hours in their lifetime helping others in the church.[11] Moreover, these six hours include family service, individual service, and youth-group service, which means experience levels are low. When training families, remember to be concrete. If you're planning a service project that entails using tools, such as hammers and saws, teach people how to use the equipment properly. Don't assume that everyone knows how to use these tools. Encourage those who do know how to use the tools to be your experts and demonstrate use of the tools to others.

• *Create meaningful service projects.* Develop projects that give each family member a sense that they can make a contribution. Recruit families who have a lot of experience in family service projects to mentor other families with little or no experience. The family mentors can help prepare another family for the volunteer experience, serve with the family, and debrief the experience with the family.

> ## MEMORABLE QUOTE
>
> "There is a call to us, a call of service—that we join with others to try to make things better in this world."
>
> Dorothy Day, cofounder of the Catholic Workers[10]

• *Offer options.* Be aware of the wide range of families that you're working with. Some will have tight schedules. Others will have more time. Some will have infants and toddlers. Some will have preschoolers. Others will have elementary-age children. Some will have teenagers. Still others will have

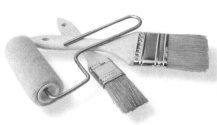

a mixture of age groups. Also offer options in terms of commitment. For families who have never done a family service project, make sure that the project is short and has immediate results (such as a one- to two-hour service project of painting a church fence or cleaning up a church yard). For families who have more experience, create service projects that challenge them, such as going to a week-long work camp.

• *Debrief the experience.* Participants need opportunities to reflect about the meaning of the service project. Develop a list of discussion questions and scriptures for families to talk about. Have questions that help families make sense of the experience, since family service projects can create both positive and negative impressions for participants.

CHURCH SPOTLIGHT

from a Sunday School class and Beyond

A ten-year-old and his family work together to plant and pick fresh vegetables at the First United Methodist Church's "The Victory Over Hunger Garden" in Framingham, Massachusetts. The mother starts the project in the spring with her Sunday school class by having the children plant the seeds and water the indoor seedlings. Starting, maintaining, and harvesting a garden is a meaningful way to get families with children of all ages involved in a worthwhile way.

Church-Based Service Projects

• *Develop an annual church yard cleanup.* Pick up trash. Plant flowers. Repair and paint old wooden fences.

• *Ask families to decorate your church sanctuary for Advent.* Children and teenagers enjoy decorating trees, windows, and other places in your church for the holidays.

• *Have families spruce-up your church nursery.* Repair or toss broken toys. Re-examine the nursery for childproofing updates. Purchase new toys.

• *Create a family ministry read-a-thon.* Raise money to buy children, teen, and family books for your church library.

• *Develop family mentors for new members of your congregation.* For example, match member families with families who are joining your church. Have your singles and older adult ministries to designate mentors for individual new members.

• *Have families create "Welcome Baskets" for new family members (either through adoption or birth) and deliver them to the families after the new family member arrives.* Welcome baskets include items for the new family member in addition to the parents and the siblings. Books, rattles, tape stories, stickers, and cookies are just a few of the items the baskets might contain.

• *Ask families to visit hospitalized members and members who are unable to leave home.* Often families are isolated from this aspect of pastoral care. If families occasionally visit these members, they learn about caring for members of the congregation they might not otherwise see.

MORE INFO

An organization About family Service

Family Matters
Points of Light Foundation
1400 Eye Street, NW, Suite 800
Washington, DC 20005
(202) 729-8000
www.pointsoflight.org
/familymatters
FAMILYMATTERS@
pointsoflight.org
This program engages families in year-round community-oriented volunteer projects. It also does research on family volunteering and sponsors an annual National Family Volunteer Day each November.

• *Have families take turns serving refreshments following a worship service or during a church event.* Young children can distribute and restock napkins. Elementary-age children can distribute and restock plastic cups as needed. Teenagers can pour coffee and juice and carry cookie trays.

Service Project Partnerships

• *Each fall, Church World Service sponsors an annual CROP Walk for Hunger.* This walkathon can appeal to all families since the only requirements are to walk outside on a weekend afternoon and secure pledges that go to help hunger efforts. Parents or siblings can pull young children in wagons, push babies in strollers, or have young children ride tricycles and bicycles while teenagers walk along with the adults. Find out more by contacting Church World Service, 28606 Phillips Street, P.O. Box 968, Elkhart, IN 46515; (800) 297-1516; cws@ncc-cusa.org; www.churchworldservice.org.

• *Link up with a Habitat affiliate near you to do a family service project.* Habitat for Humanity has more than 1,700 affiliates in all fifty states, the territories of Guam and Puerto Rico and in sixty other countries around the world. Habitat for Humanity, 121 Habitat Street, Americus, GA 31709-3498; (800) 422-4828; info@habitat.org; www.habitat.org/.

• *Join USA WEEKEND's Make a Difference Day held on the fourth Saturday in October.* Sponsored by USA WEEKEND and The Points of Light Foundation, the annual day of service gets churches, organizations, families, and individuals volunteering to make the world a better place. For more information, call 1-800-VOLUNTEER or go to the Web site www. pointsoflight.org

• *If you're creating service projects for families with junior and senior high youth, consider going on a week-long work camp through Group Workcamps.* Each year, Group Workcamps offers approximately fifty different workcamps throughout the United States. For more information, contact: Group Workcamps, Box 599, Loveland, CO 80539; (800) 774-3838; www.groupworkcamps.com.

• *Partner with human-service agencies in your community during the fall to create Christmas giving trees.* Ask the agencies to identify families within the community who would benefit by receiving an anonymous gift at Christmas. Ask for each recipient's sex (male or female), age, and two to three items on their wish list. Make a Christmas ball from construction-paper for each recipient with this information and place all the balls on a construction paper Christmas

---

FAST FACT

Barriers to Family Service

A number of barriers prohibit families from getting involved in family service activities. These include:

• coordination of time schedules within each family—48.7%;

• difficulty in including young children in volunteer projects—41.9%;

• volunteer projects are designed for individuals, not families—39.7%;

• no time to volunteer—24.5%;

• family volunteer jobs don't offer enough challenges or a variety of jobs for family members of all ages—21.7%;

• transportation difficulties—15.5%;

• insurance liability on the volunteer job site—9.4%.[12]

MEMORABLE QUOTE

"Service is the rent we pay for living. It is the very purpose of life and not something you do in your spare time."

Marian Wright Edelman,
The Measure of Our Success[13]

tree. Ask families in your church to participate in this project by having each family member select a construction paper ball and purchase a gift. Next have them tape their construction paper ball to the unwrapped gift, and place it under the construction paper tree. Then your church can deliver the gifts to the agency that distributes the gifts to the recipients.

• *Get families involved with National Youth Service Day each April through Youth Service America, an alliance of more than 200 youth-serving organizations.* Find out more through Youth Service America, 1101 15th Street, N.W., Suite 200, Washington, DC 20005; (202) 296-2992; www.servenet.org/ysa.

• *Find service and mission opportunities near you by visiting www.volunteermatch.org.* This Web site allows you to post and find volunteer opportunities near you by typing in your zip code. The Web site has church-based and secular service projects for families.

• *Scout for other service opportunities that already exist near you.* Find these by contacting a volunteer center of the United Way. Look for organizations in your phone book under social services, family services, and environmental organizations. Contact your state or region's Council of Churches or your denomination's mission board for more opportunities.

Service Projects
for All Families

• *Deliver a meal to
people who are unable to
leave home.* Talk with
them as they eat. (It's
often effective to have
one family cook the meal
and another family
deliver the meal and visit.)

• *Organize a church-wide
food drive.* Post a list of the best
nonperishable foods to give. (Your
local food bank or food shelf will have ideas.) Ask families to
bring foods.

• *Tie in Bible study whenever you do any type of service or
mission project with families.* Some scriptures worth exploring
include: Deuteronomy 10:18-19, Luke 4, Luke 12:32-34, Romans
15:25-27, and 2 Corinthians 9. Create a Bible study booklet to
accompany each service project.

• *Collect mittens, scarves, and caps during the winter for
homeless families.* Or collect children's winter coats, boots, and
snow pants for homeless children. The socks, caps, and mittens
can be hung with clothespins as decorations for a small tree.

• *Have families take turns changing your church's outdoor
sign of weekly information (if your church has a sign) or
collecting the bulletins left on pews or chairs after a worship
service.* The paper can then be recycled.

• *Ask families to bring in treats three or four times a year.*
Sunday school classes often have a snack time, and families can
contribute food for the classes their children attend.

• *Whenever your church has a collection drive, create a list
with two or three items that would be of interest to families with
children of different ages,* such as families with young children

(infants, toddlers, and preschoolers), elementary-age children, teenagers, and young adults.

• *Partner with a shelter for families or a temporary housing unit for displaced families.* Invite families to volunteer to come and play with the children for one to two hours to give parents a break and the children an opportunity to play.

• *Ask families to keep greetings cards they receive for birthdays, anniversaries, and Christmas.* Have families come together, bring all their cards, and see how many pounds of cards your church has collected. Send the cards to St. Jude's Ranch, 100 St. Jude's Street, Boulder City, NV 89005 where the children recycle the cards to make new ones.

Service Projects for Families with Young Children

<table>
<tr><td>

BONUS IDEA

A Good Ride

Link families who have transporta-tion with individuals or families in your congregation who don't.

Have families with transporta-tion run errands or take people to appointments once a month.

</td><td>

• *Collect toys for young children who are either hospitalized, in foster care, or in a crisis nursery.* Collect toys such as rattles, puzzles, stuffed animals, blocks, balls, musical tapes, and board books.

• *Have families with young children visit with people who rarely see children.* Visit hos-pices, nursing homes, assisted-living facilities, or families with church members unable to leave home. Young

</td></tr>
</table>

children have a spontaneity and optimistic attitude that can often uplift any spirit.

• *Ask families to make May baskets (out of construction paper) and fill the baskets with candy and small toys.* (Some parents order kid's meals at fast-food restaurants and then keep the toy to use for service project collections.) Have families deliver the May baskets anonymously on May Day (May 1st) to neighbors with children. Young children can put stickers and stars on the construction-paper baskets to decorate them.

• *Invite families to sort through their children's outgrown shoes and clothes.* Create goody bags with these items for other families in your church who have children growing into those clothes.

CHURCH SPOTLIGHT

A Large Welcome for Babies

Families at Good Shepherd Lutheran Church in Oak Park, Illinois, deliver meals to every church family with a newborn. "It's a big adjustment time to begin with," says the mother of two who coordinates the program. "Families of newborns don't need the extra hassle of preparing dinners." In addition to delivering meals, families doing the project also spend time visiting and getting to know the family with the newborn.[14]

• *Have families with young children draw pictures and make greeting cards for people in your congregation who are sick.* Ask the families to hand deliver the cards and pictures so they can visit with sick members if it is appropriate.

• *Create a cheerleading service project where families with young children attend one sporting event in which your church participates.* (Your church may have a softball, basketball, or bowling league, for example.) Have children clap, shout "hooray" and "Go-Go-GO," and show their support. Consider having families dress alike; for example, have families dress in matching shirts or have the children all wear Dalmatian spots and shout "We spot a good sport."

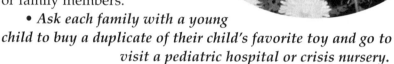

• *If your church lawn or nearby park has lots of dandelions, have families with young children go dandelion picking (with the goal of getting every single dandelion).* Then make dandelion bouquets to give to church staff, neighbors, or family members.

• *Ask each family with a young child to buy a duplicate of their child's favorite toy and go to visit a pediatric hospital or crisis nursery.* Have families take both the new and the old toy when they visit and allow the children to play together. Then give the new toy to the hospitalized child. Young children love giving a toy that they also have so that they can be "the same."

• *Have families with young children give a "shower of thanks" to your senior pastor, church secretary, children's ministry, Christian education coordinator, or nursery caregiver.* Invite families to make thank-you cards to send or decorate the recipient's office when you know the person will be away. With young children, use crepe paper and hand-drawn pictures as decorations, rather than balloons.

• *Ask families to volunteer to work at water stops and food booths for marathon races and walkathons.* Young children love filling up cups with water or other beverages.

Services Project for Families with Elementary-Age Children

- *Offer a dog wash in your church parking lot on a summer weekend afternoon.* Designate money raised to go to a worthy cause. Create charges by the dog's size (small, medium, or large) or by the pound (use a bathroom scale). Have families with younger elementary-age children soap, wash, and rinse off the dogs with a garden hose. Have families with older elementary-age children use hair dryers and rags to dry off the dogs.
- *Have families offer home-care services for members going on vacation or on a business trip.* People who travel often look for someone to care for their pets and plants, pick up their mail and newspaper, and check on their home. Elementary-age children (with the supervision of a parent) enjoy serving others in this way.
- *Invite families to volunteer during a preschool Sunday school class.* Families can lead a fifteen -

---

FAST FACT

Why families Serve Together

Congregations and other organizations that create family service projects say these are the top reasons families volunteer:

- it gives the opportunity to teach values of service and community involvement—70.8%;

- there's a social responsibility to give back to the community—56.7%;

- it provides an opportunity for the parent or extended family to be involved with the younger generation—56.7%;

- it gives an opportunity for family members to get to know one another better as they serve—53.4%;

- it's a traditional way for families to serve—35.0%;

- it's a cultural, religious, or ethnic tradition—32.9%;

- it saves time to work together—25.3%.[15]

minute music time, fifteen-minute craft time, or a fifteen-minute story time .

- *Ask the church council to designate a small space for a family-run church garden.* Have families research different types of perennials and annual flowers that would be ideal the amount of sun and shade the plot will have. Families can then plant seeds and seedlings. Or grow vegetables that can be given to a local foodbank or soup kitchen. Have families sign up for times to weed, fertilize, water, and care for the plants.

- *Have families cut out grocery coupons to give to a local food bank.* Elementary-age children enjoy cutting and collecting.

- *Make gift baskets for a nearby nursing home or assisted-care facility for older adults.* Before you begin, call and ask for permission to make gift baskets. Find out about any special needs and visiting hours. Then have families assemble gift baskets with personal care items (such as toothbrushes, toothpaste, and combs), food (such as fruit, crackers, and candy), large-print books, activities (such as a deck of cards and Dominoes), and writing supplies (such as stationery, pens, tablets of paper, postage stamps, and envelopes). After the baskets have been assembled, deliver them in person so that families can spend time getting to know the recipient.

- *Schedule a time for families to hold and rock babies in a hospital nursery.* Get permission first.

- *Be welcoming attendants as a family at a shelter or a drop-in center.* Many of these places need volunteers to sign people in, distribute blankets and towels (or other items), and give newcomers a tour of the facilities. With more families using shelters and drop-in centers, having families to welcome them helps them feel less afraid and awkward.

• *Have families volunteer to rescue food that's leftover at a special event, at restaurants, bakeries, and/or hospitals.* Ask them to deliver the food to soup kitchens and homeless shelters that serve meals. Often thousands of pounds of food go to waste because food-rescue programs don't have enough volunteers to help pick up and deliver the food. To connect with a food rescue organization near you, contact the Food Chain National Food Rescue Organization at (800) 845-3008.

• *Have families volunteer to stuff a church bulletin or assist with a large mailing for your church.* Children can help stuff and seal envelopes while adults can ensure that folding and mail labels are done accurately.

Service Projects for Families with Teenagers and Young Adults

• *Coach a sports team for young children.* Many community parks and recreation departments offer basketball, soccer, and baseball (or T-ball) leagues for elementary-age children who are learning the basic skills of a sport.

• *Speak out about social issues in your community.* Encourage families to write letters to the editor for your local newspaper.

• *Use more in-depth skills to create items for people in need.* For example, some families have strong carpentry skills and can erect wooden fences or build household items, such as cupboards and bookshelves. Other families who do a lot of sewing can make quilts for mission projects.

• *For families who like to travel and serve, Habitat for Humanity has the Global Village program.* Families can travel to countries within Africa, Latin America, the Caribbean, Asia, and North America to build houses while also seeing the sights. Contact the Global Village Department at (800) HABITAT, ext. 2549, www.habitat.org, or E-mail gv@hfhi.org.

• *Have a group take a long bike ride (such as for one hundred miles or from one end of your state to the other) to raise funds for a worthy cause.* Or organize a jogging trek, walking adventure, or canoe trip.

• *Form a family welcoming committee that reaches out to families who join your church.* Get to know these families. Give them information about how to become assimilated in your church community. Have welcoming families make a one-year commitment to go out of their way to see and build relationships with new members.

• *Collect slightly used musical instruments.* Give these instruments to children who want to learn to play an instrument but whose families don't have the financial resources to purchase it.

• *For families with teenagers and young adults who are adept at working with cars, offer a free car tune-up for people in your church.* Do simple auto repair and oil changes.

• *Tutor a young child.* Help a child learn English as a second language, learn how to read, or master another subject.

• *Have a family or a group of two to three families develop a youth or adult forum.* Families can choose a specific topic of interest, such as hunger or homelessness.

Chapter 5

Welcoming Worship

creating family-friendly Services

A Colorado church invites everyone to the table for communion—including children who haven't received first communion. While adults, teenagers, and older children receive the cup and bread, younger children are given a few grapes and a cracker. Church leaders made this change when they learned the struggles families faced while trying to explain to young children why they couldn't participate. Now whole families eat and drink at the table together. No one is left out. Everyone in the congregation knows and celebrates the significance of when older children move from getting grapes and crackers to receiving the cup and bread.

Being intentional about including families in worship entails examining the experience from the pew rather than from the pulpit. Until recently, many churches were satisfied with how they meet the needs of families by doing children's sermons in traditional services and adding contemporary services to their worship lineup. Yet if you scrutinize the makeup of traditional and contemporary services, you'll

FAST FACT

Uplifting Worship Services

Of the adults surveyed in six major mainline denominations, 70 percent rate their congregations as excellent or good in providing spiritually uplifting worship services, according to Search Institute researchers.[1]

MEMORABLE QUOTE

"Worship is not only a place to dream and envi-sion a 'new heaven and a new earth' where the deaf hear, the blind see, and outcasts come to a feast; worship is also a time set apart to focus our attention on and attach ourselves to something and someone outside ourselves."

William H. Willimon,
The Service of God [2]

find families at both. You'll also find middle-aged people and older adults at both. It's time we rethink traditional and contemporary worship services to better meet the needs of families.

In many ways, St. Luke Presbyterian Church in Wayzata, Minnesota, has done this. Name tags for all worship participants (including children, teenagers, and adults) hang in the narthex. Families are readers, greeters, ushers, musicians, and dancers. Sometimes family members will give a responsive reading. A folk choir of family members sings about once a month. A Christmas pageant, which is a re-enactment of the Christmas story, includes four-year-old angels singing "Away in a Manger" and teenagers playing the parts of Mary, Joseph, and the other central characters. The newest member of the church—the one born closest to Christmas—gets to be Jesus. During the pageant, families sing traditional Christmas songs together and step forward and place their offering in the empty manger while Mary, Joseph, and the baby smile at them. In the spring, families work together to put on a musical play during a worship service. A musician in the church writes the musical and creates parts with the wide age range in mind.

Passing on the faith to families through worship involves seeing each family member as an active participant each Sunday, not just on Mother's Day, Father's Day, and Youth Sunday. It means creating ways to engage the wiggly preschoolers, the sleepy teenagers, and the often-  stressed parents who have come to nurture their souls and build their faith. It requires a sensitivity to bring-  ing families together rather than separating them, which churches typically overlook by gearing children's ser- mons for children and the main sermon for adults. It's not easy to create family-friendly worship services; but when we're creative and faithful, we can create worship experiences that nurture the faith of every family member.

Family Involvement in Worship

• *Have families take turns making the weekly worship announcements*. In addition to getting families more involved in worship, this also helps them feel as if the church is "their" church instead of "those people's" church. Sometimes families feel as if the church belongs to the church leadership since family members often are unable to devote much time to church activities.

• *Invite families to read the lesson or part of the liturgy*. Families can break up a reading and do it responsively, or differ- ent family members can read different parts. For example, one family member could read the first lesson, another the second les- son, and a third the Gospel.

MORE INFO

Family-friendly Worship

Forbid Them Not: Involving Children in Sunday Worship, Years A, B, and C by Carolyn C. Brown (Nashville: Abingdon Press, 1993, 1994) shows how to create meaningful worship services that include children and families, based on the Revised Common Lectionary.

• *Recruit families to be greeters and to distribute worship bulletins as people enter the sanctuary.* Consider having children and teenagers hand out the children's bulletin, if your church has one.

• *If your church has attendance registers for members to sign, encourage families to have each of their children sign the register.* This helps children and teenagers feel like valued members of your worship service.

• *Create a focus group of families from your church to offer feedback about what they like and dislike about worship.* Incorporate some of their family-friendly ideas.

• *Have families participate in worship through music and the arts.* See chapter 7 for ideas about how to do this.

• *If your worship service uses acolytes, consider having a family fill this role periodically.*

• *Ask family members (and other church members) to wear clothing of the appropriate color to celebrate different seasons of the church year.* Wear white for Epiphany, red for Pentecost, black for Good Friday, white for Easter, and purple for Advent.

• *By following your religious tradition, consider how families can assist with serving Communion.* Maybe children and teenagers can pick up the empty cups (if that's in your tradition), or perhaps they can walk with their parents as their parents assist with the distribution.

• *Have families be ushers.* Pair family members together to guide the passing of the offering plate.

• *Create an annual family worship service.* (Some churches have a youth Sunday each year, which can provide a model.) Incorporate creative ways for families to lead and participate in this service to celebrate families.

Worship Accessories

• *Recruit your church sewing circle (or individuals who enjoy sewing) to make soft-bodied worship dolls, cloth books, or lap quilts for children to use during worship services.*

• *Distribute children's worship bulletins.* An Ohio company creates weekly children's worship bulletins, one for ages three to six and another for children ages seven to twelve. Contact: CRI, 4150 Belden Village Street, Fourth Floor, Canton, OH 44718; (800) 992-2144; www.childrensbulletins.com.

• *Find ways to offer simple items for family members to hold and use during worship, such as a star on Epiphany Sunday, a palm branch on Palm Sunday, or a nail on Good Friday.* Making worship concrete helps not only the children but also the adults better understand the message.

• *Include small pieces of writing paper in your pew racks (if your church has them) along with sharpened pencils.* This allows antsy children to write or draw during the sermon.

CHURCH SPOTLIGHT

Teaching Children How to Worship

Families with first graders get to attend an "open house" each September at Bedford Presbyterian Church in Bedford, New Hampshire. At the open house, children and parents learn to worship through a simulation worship service. First the church leaders lead families through a worship service without a plan. Participants pray, listen to the pastor, sing, give their offerings, and read the Bible lessons all at the same time. Usually at the end of this experience, everyone is laughing.

(continued on the next page)

• *Create a scriptural booklet about why your church worships God.* Consider including scriptures, such as 1 Chronicles 16:8-36, Psalm 99, Luke 4:1-13, John 4:19-24, and Hebrews 12:28-29.

• *Set up a display in the narthex of Christian picture books and novels for children.* Encourage families to pick up one or two books before the service for children to look at and read during the worship service. Some congregations allow family members to check out books for a certain period of time.

• *Create worship bags with activities for young children.* Saint Stephen Lutheran Church in Bloomington, Minnesota, designed rainbow bags that have creative activities for children, such as puppets of biblical characters, Christian coloring pages, crayons, plain paper, and a few pencils. A large wooden rainbow with pegs hold the cloth bags in the narthex for children to pick up before worship.[3]

• *Develop a simplified worship bulletin for children and teenagers that includes the order of your worship service, the actual readings (so they don't have to look through books of worship), and the words to hymns.* Get permission from the copyright holders of the books and hymns to print the selections (usually obtaining permission is easy and free). Simplifying the worship bulletin is a great way to teach family members about the order of worship and the ways they can participate.

• *Periodically create a flyer giving more information about a specific element of worship, such as a flyer about offering or hymns or sermons or prayers.* You could include fun historical facts about the element and thought-provoking tips for families to consider.

Church Spotlight
(continued)

Then the church leaders explain the order of worship and show how all the elements of worship fall into four categories:

• singing to God,

• praying to God,

• listening to God's word,

• giving to God.

Church leaders then act out different parts of the worship service, and families guess which of the four categories the part fits into. Families can experience the organ up close through a demonstration by the organist. Families are also taught how to use the worship bulletin and to follow along with the service.[4]

• *Occasionally ask families to share their family faith stories with the congregation during a worship service.* For example, have a family active in family service projects relate their experiences. Or find a family that is diligent about giving an offering and has all of their children giving money each week as part of their weekly faith ritual.

Worship Ideas for Different Church Seasons

• *Have families wrap their offering envelopes (including their children's if they have individual offering envelopes) in one of the solid foil wraps (such as red, green, blue, gold, or silver) for Epiphany Sunday.* Invite families to process to an offering basket at the front of your church (or to a crèche) while singing "We Three Kings."

• *Celebrate baptism.* On the first Sunday after Epiphany, which typically celebrates Jesus' baptism, include in your worship service a time for family members to walk to the baptismal font or tank and dip their fingers or hands into the water to remind them of their baptism or to show them what's to come when they will be baptized.

• *During the worship service on Transfiguration Sunday, ask family members to write on a piece of paper one thing that they would like to change about themselves.* (Encourage parents to help children who haven't learned how to write.) Ideas could include being more kind, giving more money to good causes, attending a Bible study, praying on a daily basis, and so on. Then have family members fold the papers and place them in the offering plate along with their offerings.

• *Since many families find it difficult to attend all the worship services during Holy Week, create times of the day when family members can stop, pray, and remember the significance of the particular day of this important week.* Create a short devotional for the Monday of Holy Week, the Tuesday of Holy Week, the Wednesday of Holy Week, Maundy Thursday, Good Friday, and the Saturday of Holy Week.

• *Have each family bring a red candle to light and place on the altar to celebrate Pentecost.*

• *Invite a creative family to design a dramatic reading of Acts 2:1-13 for Pentecost.* For example, family members could blow like the wind, repeat the word "fire" at opportune times, and talk all at the same time (but with different words or in different languages). Or create this type of reading that all worship participants can do together.

MEMORABLE QUOTE

"Children like to talk, and they're always wiggling— so a good children's message should let kids talk and wiggle."

Donald Hinchey, *5-Minute Messages for Children*[5]

• *One of the longest seasons of the church is the season after Pentecost.* Some church traditions call this "ordinary time," so during this season consider celebrating what's ordinary about life. For example, ask members of each family to bring an object that symbolizes what they cherish about ordinary life, such as a rock, a feather, a stick, a postage stamp, or a pencil, to place on the altar.

• *If your church has a decorated tree for the Advent and Christmas season, consider making the tree decorating part of a worship service during Advent.* Give each family an ornament as they enter the sanctuary for the worship service; then have a time when families come forward to hang their ornament on the tree.

• *Have families take turns lighting the candles in the Advent wreath each Sunday.* If you have many families, recruit a different family to light each candle each Sunday. For example, on the third Sunday of Advent, have three different

families each light one candle. That way ten families—instead of four—can participate in the lighting of the Advent wreath candles.

• *Many churches traditionally have a Christmas Eve candlelight service late in the evening of December 24th.* This is typically too late for families, especially those with young children. Consider adding a family Christmas Eve service in the late afternoon (such as at 4:00) in addition to your 10:00 P.M. or 11:00 P.M. service. Even if you have a small congregation, you can often attract to a family Christmas Eve service many people from your community who typically don't attend church.

Children's Sermons

• *Have a sermon about relationships.* Invite children to bring one adult with them during this children's sermon.

• *Consider having a seasoned preschool teacher give the children's sermon occasionally.* A teacher will typically come up with a unique topic and a message that's developmentally appropriate for children.

• *Give to each child attending a children's sermon an item to take to their parents, such as a carnation or a red heart.* Note: If you want children to give away something to eat (such as a chocolate kiss), give each child two, one to eat and one to give.

• *For a children's sermon, recruit enough adults and teenagers beforehand so that each one can bring a child from the church nursery to your children's sermon.* You could have these young children be part of your message or just be hearers of the message. This is a way to include very young children for a brief time in your worship service and also to show worship participants the number of infants and toddlers your church has (which they otherwise may never see). Preschoolers and elementary-age children listening to the children's sermon also enjoy seeing infants and toddlers.

• *Hold the children's sermon in different parts of your sanctuary, such as in the balcony, near the altar, near the pulpit, in a pew, and so on.* As long as the person giving the sermon has a microphone or a voice that projects well, be creative about where you give children's sermons.

Church Nurseries

• *Invest in families. Hire child-care providers to run your church nursery during worship services.* Although this may seem like an unnecessary, luxurious cost, parents looking for a church to join (and those deciding whether or not to stay) are very aware of the quality of service a church nursery provides. Plus, hired providers mean that you have more consistent, reliable, trained caregivers and you don't need to scramble for volunteers.

• *Wire speakers in the church nursery so that nursery workers can hear the worship service while they're providing care in the nursery.* This helps nursery workers to feel less isolated from the service.

• *Periodically create processionals (such as carrying palms on Palm Sunday) that include parents with young children so that they can come into the church together and sing one short hymn (or a hymn with one to two verses).* Afterward, give parents time to leave briefly (while the congregation sings another hymn or sings additional verses of the processional hymn) to take their children to the nursery before returning to worship.

• *Give your worship committee and worship leaders a tour of your church nursery.* This is often what families with young children see first when coming to a worship service. What are their reactions? How can worship leaders include the church nursery as part of their thinking when designing worship services?

• *Incorporate a prayer time and a song time into the church nursery so that even the youngest of your church's children get to participate in (or at least observe) prayers and songs.*

Prayers, Offerings, and Readings

• *Give each family a bubble solution container with a bubble blowing wand in it.* Create a prayer or reading that emphasizes the many good things that God gives. During certain parts of the prayer or reading, have families blow bubbles so that the sanctuary is filled with bubbles.

• *Have a reverse offering.* Fill up the offering plates with pennies. Pass them around the church and encourage each person to take one penny. Talk about how God gives us many great things, even though they may seem small and we take them for granted. Emphasize how God gives us things *every day* and yet an offering plate comes around only once a week.

• *When creating responsive readings, instead of creating parts for people by age and gender* (such as for children, teenagers, adults, men, and women), create parts for different types of families, such as for families with children, for families with teenagers, for families with adult children, for singles, and so on. Creating readings in which family members can read parts together helps build family cohesiveness.

BONUS IDEA

family-friendly Worship Bulletins

Include pictures (or symbols) in your church bulletin next to each item of the worship service to show nonreading (and parents who are unsure) what happens next. Use praying hands next to prayers, music notes next to hymns, a dollar sign next to the offering, an ear next to the sermon. Use a star next to items for times you want people to stand and nothing for times people can sit.

• *Create a visible prayer chain for your sanctuary.* Give each family member a 1-inch by 6-inch piece of colored construction paper. During the service, have family members write their names on the pieces of paper. (Encourage parents to help children who aren't old enough to write so those children are included.) Have ushers collect the colored construction paper and assemble them into paper chains. Either at the end of the service or by the next week's service, display the paper prayer chains in your sanctuary. Talk about how each person counts in your church and about how each person is prayed for.

• *Give each family member entering the sanctuary a dandelion, wildflower, or some other inexpensive flower (like a daisy).* During the service, have family members process to the altar and say, "Thank you, God" as they place their flower into empty vases on the altar. After everyone has finished, talk about how the little things we give multiply and become beautiful, large bouquets of giving.

• **Create a prayer that emphasizes what family members do with their hands.** During the prayer, have family members stand and do the actions. Include items such as these: "God, sometimes we feel like we don't have enough so we clench our hands to hang on to the little we have (clench hands). We become worried and don't know what to do (place hands on both cheeks). Help us to open our hands (open hands). Help us to give (have one hand pick an imaginary item from the other hand and give it). Help us to reach out to each other (hold hands with family members)."

• **Create a litany of confession** *where everyone responds after each sentence by saying, "Have mercy on us."* Include lines such as: "God, we often think we don't need our families." "Open our hearts so we can love each other more deeply." "Help us heal the wounds in our families." "Open our ears so we can hear more clearly." "Help us to know when to speak the truth in love and when to bite our tongues." "Open our minds to learn from each other." "Help us be present with each other." "Amen."

• **Give a cut-out heart shape to each member as they enter the sanctuary.** Before the offering, have each member write the name of one person in their nuclear and extended families that they wish they felt more loving toward. After people finish, have them fold their hearts in half and place them in the offering plate with their offerings.

• *Give each family member a sticky note as they enter the sanctuary.* During the service, ask people to write one prayer request on their note and then process forward and place it on the pulpit, altar, or other visible place in your sanctuary.

• *Create a reading about families and family relationships based on the scriptures about families.* See the sidebar "Family Issues in Scripture" in chapter 2 (starting on page 28) for ideas.

Additional Ideas for Families and Worship

• *Occasionally have parenting commissioning services to commission parents in their important role as their child enters a new stage in life.* Do this in the fall with parents of newborns, parents of kindergartners, parents of children entering middle school for the first time, parents with teenagers starting high school for the first time, and parents sending off their children to college. Mark these important transition times for families.

• *Examine other times to have worship services so that families can worship together.* With more people working on Sunday mornings and sport teams scheduling games on Sundays, many families are finding that their schedules conflict with Sunday worship. One church added a Wednesday evening worship service; another added a Friday evening worship service; yet another started a Sunday evening service.

> **MORE INFO**
>
> Giving Better Children Sermons
>
>
>
> *5-Minute Messages and More,* by Donald Hinchey (Loveland, Colo.: Group Books, 1998) features Bible-based sermons that really captivate children's attention and imagination. Donald Hinchey has written three other books of children's sermons also published by Group Books.

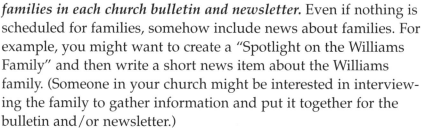

- *Have a blessings of the animals ceremony during which families can bring their pets to a short, outdoor service.* Children enjoy showing others their pets, and this type of service gives families the chance to connect in new ways.

- *Be intentional about including family activities, family educational workshops, and other announcements for families in each church bulletin and newsletter.* Even if nothing is scheduled for families, somehow include news about families. For example, you might want to create a "Spotlight on the Williams Family" and then write a short news item about the Williams family. (Someone in your church might be interested in interviewing the family to gather information and put it together for the bulletin and/or newsletter.)

- *Create new pledge cards for stewardship Sunday.* Either encourage everyone to make a pledge (including children and teenagers) or create a pledge card for families that includes blanks for children and teenagers to also make their pledges. Emphasize that giving isn't just for families to do as a unit but also for individual family members. Then have entire families process forward and place their pledge cards in baskets or offering plates on the altar.

- *During a worship service when it's not too cold, have family members take off their shoes when they enter the sanctuary.* Ask them to line up their shoes so that the shoes are pointing toward the exit of the sanctuary. During the service, emphasize how worship helps us to stand tall so that we can walk into the world and be Christian witnesses.

• *In some churches, young people preparing to be confirmed take "sermon notes" on the weekly sermon.* Consider occasionally distributing a "sermon note" sheet and encouraging families to take notes on the messages of the service. Point out that hymns, prayers, and readings—in addition to the sermon—give messages to people in worship.

• *On Mother's Day and Father's Day, provide ways to recognize the parents in your worship service while also learning more about them.* For example, on Mother's Day, bring a dozen, long-stemmed roses (or red carnations if you have a small budget). Ask for mothers to raise their hands (and receive one single flower if they meet one of the following criteria) for: having the most children, having the youngest child in the congregation, having the oldest child in the congregation, having children closest together in age, having children farthest apart in age, having twins (or triplets), adopting a child who originally lived the farthest away, being a foster parent to the most children, having the most boys, having the most girls, parenting living in a home closest to your church, and parenting living in a home farthest from your church.

• *When giving a message about the feeding of the five thousand, show families part of this story.* Bring a loaf of bread (or more depending on the size of your congregation) and ask each person to take a bit of the bread to eat before passing it to the next person in the pew. Have the bread distributed throughout the entire church and then have the leftovers brought to you when everyone has finished. Talk about how as families we often feel that what we have will never meet our needs;

but that in reality when we make good choices, God meets our needs and often there is something left over.

• *Find a puzzle that has a picture of a church or a cathedral on it.* Set up a table in the narthex for the puzzle to be put together. As family members come to worship, give each person a puzzle piece. Explain that sometimes when we come to church, we don't know how we fit in. After the service, encourage families to bring their puzzle pieces to the table in the narthex. Serve beverages and cookies in that area to encourage people to hang around until the puzzle is completed.

CHURCH SPOTLIGHT

An Alternative Family Worship Service

Trinity Episcopal Church in Menlo Park, California, has created an alternative worship service for families. At this service, rugs are placed in front of the church along with small chairs so that children and their families can sit in front in a more informal manner. This encourages young children to be more engaged in the service since they're sitting up front.

The next week, refer to the puzzle during the worship service.

• *When your church does a service or mission project that encourages people to bring items (such as food for a shelter), designate a worship service to emphasize this.* Encourage people to bring an item to that particular worship service and set the item on the altar. Often this boosts the number of items brought in, and the project becomes more meaningful when it's tied to worship.

Chapter 6

Congregational Care

Supporting Families

Supporting families means more than providing encouragement and care through their faith journey. It also means empowering families to build their own resources, supports, and strengths. "It involves respecting the needs, aspirations, and goals families have identified, rather than imposing your pastoral care or programs on them," write Richard P. Olson and Joe H. Leonard in *A New Day for Family Ministry*. "To minister within a framework of family support means two things: (1) *listening to what families say* about their lives, hopes, and needs; and (2) *believing in the capacity of Christians to reach out to one another* in powerfully caring ways."[1] To support families in empowering ways entails knowing what they need and also what they aspire to. To do that requires building relationships with families.

Clergy and paid church staff aren't the only ones who can build relationships with families. The entire congregation can. In fact, building relationships with families is more effective when everyone is involved. When we move from a mentality of pastoral care to congregational

FAST FACT

The Main Benefit of Support Groups

A survey of support group participants found that the main reason people liked these groups was because they made people feel like they weren't alone.[3]

care, we empower each member of the congregation to take an active part in ministry.

In a survey of congregations, researchers found that a warm, welcoming, and friendly climate is a key quality of a faith-enhancing congregation.[2] "Indeed, climate may have as much influence on why people come to and stay in church as do specific programs offered," the authors of the report concluded.[4] When we create a community of care within a congregation, family members will more likely feel that their needs are met and that they belong to a church with caring people.

Asking people in the congregation to build relationships with families is a way to tap into each person's needs: *the need to connect* and *the need for community*. While some people may feel shy about talking to people they don't know, deep down people have the sense that they want to be part of a caring congregation. People feel welcome and connected when they walk into a congregation where someone knows their name or waves hello. They feel left out when they attend a church where no one seems to notice whether they're there or not.

Traditionally, churches tend to think of support groups and sending an occasional card as the main ways to support families. While these two ways are supportive gestures, there are many more ways to make your congregation a caring, supportive place for families. By opening up possibilities for different ways to care for families, we can help family members feel more connected to our churches and to each other.

Easy Ideas to Support Families

• *Learn the names of each family member, including the children and teenagers.* Greet family members by name whenever you see them.

• *Make sure your youth and children's programs aren't overplanned.* Consider setting aside one night per week as "family night" where no committee meetings or church activities are allowed to be scheduled. Families need time to spend together at home.

• *List each family member in your church directory, including children, teenagers, and other family members who don't attend your church.* Even if only one family member comes to a church, emphasize that it's helpful for members to know about the person's family so that the congregation can support the person by knowing about the significant people in his or her life.

• *Celebrate holidays that are related to families.* Honor Mother's Day and Father's Day. Celebrate National Family Week. A number of Christian churches mark this event the first full week of May, celebrating the week with a kick-off on the first Sunday in May.

• *Give each family member (including children and teenagers) a permanent name tag to wear to church each Sunday.* Encourage the congregation to wear their name tags so that people can begin to learn each other's names. Even if you have a small congregation where most people know each other, emphasize that families visiting the church for the first time will feel more welcome if everyone wears a name tag.

• *On New Year's, encourage families to write "family care" or "family faith care" resolutions.* These could include having a family day once a week (or once a month), having a family Bible study, or talking about faith issues when the family watches a movie or TV together.

• *Accept and affirm each family's involvement in your church, even if it's minimal.* Focus on what families are doing right, instead of what they're doing wrong.

• *Create a family-friendly, warm climate within your church.* This means that everyone in your church adopts a friendly attitude to other members and visitors.

• *When family members bring extended family members and friends to church, go out of your way to meet these people.* Get to know the grandparents, aunts, uncles, and friends of families in your church—even if these people come only periodically and are members elsewhere.

MORE INFO

A Family Support Resource

Helping Children by Strengthening Families: A Look at Family Support Programs (Washington, D.C.: Children's Defense Fund, 1992) highlights key ways to support and strengthen families.

• Occasionally call, E-mail, or drop a note to a family. Let them know you're thinking about them.

Ideas for Supporting Entire Families

• At church-wide fellowship gatherings, designate a photographer to take pictures. Make double prints and post one set on a bulletin board (or use them in a church newsletter). Give the other copy to the family in the picture. People appreciate receiving pictures of their family.

• Pair families of new members with families who have been members for awhile.

CHURCH SPOTLIGHT

Supporting Marriages

The Center for Family Ministry at St. Charles Pastoral Center in Romeoville, Illinois, has a Wedding Anniversary Mass and Renewal of Marriage Vows each year. The event is held in late summer, and all couples renew their marriage vows. The center also encourages congregations to celebrate World Marriage Day, which is the second Sunday in February.

Encourage long-term members to think of themselves as shepherding families who are to: go out of their way to greet and talk to the new family at church services and events, guide the family in getting acquainted with the programs and services of your church, and contact the family to let them know they're missed when they're absent from worship or other church-wide events.

• Create baby baskets to bring to families after the birth or the adoption of a child. Include items with each family member in mind, such as a book for an older child, a gift certificate to a local family restaurant, and something for the newest family member.

• *Have an intergenerational, family-centered vacation Bible school (VBS) during the summer.* Bethel Lutheran Church in Northfield, Minnesota, created a VBS program where adults, children, and teenagers learned side by side.

• *Connect families whenever you can.* For example, parents of a one-year-old can be connected with parents of a newborn. Encourage blended families who have been together for a number of years to support a new blended family.

• *Create a family Bible study where family members study about being a family together.* For example, Jesus often used the analogy of the parent-child relationship to show how God related to people of faith. Study Matthew 5:45-48 and Matthew 7:7-11.

• *Find out about families that belong to more than one church or faith tradition.* (For example, you may have a family with a Jewish father and a Christian mother or another family with a Protestant father and a Catholic mother.) Develop ways to support families that are honoring different faith traditions by respecting the family and the different faiths.

• *Let people know about the family resources that are available in your church.* For example, some churches have a family ministry committee. Give families the names and phone numbers of committee members along with meeting times, dates, and places. A few churches even have a designated family minister, while others divide that responsibility among the church staff and/or lay leaders. Give families clear information about who is responsible for particular ministry areas.

• *Learn what families are looking for in your church.* Most come to church with specific needs and hopes. Find out what their expectations are so that you can better meet their needs.

• *Have a family spotlight in your church newsletter or church bulletin each week.* Ask a church member to interview a family and discover more about each family member and what the family likes to do together. Then print (with permission) the information in your church newsletter or bulletin.

MEMORABLE QUOTE

"Perhaps as never before, the church needs to be a place of renewal and support for families."

Jim Larson, *A Church Guide for Strengthening Families*[5]

Ideas for Supporting Individual Family Members

• *Create "prayer pals" or "faith partners" so that each child and teenager in your church is connected with an adult outside of their immediate and extended family.* During welcome-back Sunday in the fall, publicize this program, emphasizing that it is a low-key, low-commitment program where partners are to pray for each other, send occasional cards, and go out of their way to greet each other during church gatherings.

• *Start an "It's Amazing!" bulletin board.* Subscribe to newsletters and newspapers from local schools (elementary, middle school, and senior high), child-care centers, and communities of your congregational members. Clip stories and pictures of individual family

BONUS IDEA

Set Up a Regular Family Visitation Schedule

Create a one-, two-, or three-year visitation cycle of all the families in your church so that every family is visited once at home on a regular basis. This not only shows families that you care but it also gives you the chance to build more intimate relationships with families and get their feedback about how your church can more effectively meet their needs.

members and post them on the bulletin board. (Encourage members to also send in clippings and pictures from office newsletters and other sources that you may not have access to.) Replace the postings each month. Give the originals to the families along with a personal note of congratulations.

• *Encourage teachers and youth group leaders to get to know each child and teenager personally so that young people have a caring adult in the church who supports them.* Then identify ways for parents to be known personally so they also can be cared for. One way to do this is to have the parents of a class or youth group get together for activities so that parents can get to know each other. Then have parents form shepherd pairs (or trios) with the purpose of caring for each other.

• *Recognize a "star of the week" from among the children and teenagers in your congregation.* (Or you may want to feature two to three people each week if you have a large number of young people. Make sure to recognize each young person between September and May.) If you have a large congregation, recognize a "family of the week." Create a star name tag

for the young person or for each member of a recognized family to wear. Have someone in your congregation interview the person and write a brief article about the person for the church bulletin and newsletter. During worship, recognize the person or family and encourage people to greet the person or family after the service.

• *Find out the significant dates and anniversaries of family members.* Learn about people's birthdays, adoption arrival dates, adoption finalization dates, marriage anniversaries, death anniversaries (of a significant family member). Mark these important dates somehow.

• *As part of teacher training for your Christian education program, encourage teachers to get to know their students as individuals and to build relationships with them.* Some teachers take students on occasional field trips as a way of doing some creative teaching while getting to know their students in a different setting. Others add relationship-building activities to their curriculum. A number of teachers periodically send notes, make personal phone calls, or visit each child's home throughout the year.

CHURCH SPOTLIGHT

Supporting Working Parents

Westwood Lutheran Church in St. Louis Park, Minnesota, offers mini camps for working parents on school holidays throughout the year. On days that school is out (such as during fall break, Martin Luther King Jr.'s birthday, and President's Day) the church offers mini education camps for a fee. The mini camp lasts from 8:30 A.M. to 4:30 P.M. and includes lunch for first-through sixth-graders. Children learn Bible stories and discover more about their faith (thus making it a Christian education experience) while also getting to know their peers at church by spending a longer period of time with them.

• ***Develop a parent network in your church.*** Often churches have strong avenues for supporting children and youth (through education and youth group programs) but nothing for parents. Consider having a parent network coordinator for your church to identify and get to know all the parents of children and youth in your church. That person can then determine specific ways to support parents.

• *When nonfamily members in your church begin to know the children, youth, and parents of the congregation, encourage them to attend concerts, games, or other events of individual family members to show their support.* Some churches even publish in their church newsletter or bulletin when young people are performing in a school play, giving a school concert, or playing in a game, inviting members to attend.

MORE INFO

Building Community for Families

Sharing the Journey: Support Groups and America's New Quest for Community by Robert Wuthnow (New York, Free Press, 1994) gives a comprehensive view of how to build community for people through support groups and other groups.

• *Find out where working parents are employed.* Sometimes you can create a supportive group to get together by work location. (Or if you have a number of members in a metropolitan area, they can have a monthly lunch at a restaurant.)

• *Learn what interests individual family members have.* Bring people together around those interests. For example, your church may create a writing group for parents who are interested in writing, a rappelling group for parents who enjoy climbing, or a model-car-making group for interested children and youth.

Supporting Families in Transition and Crisis

• *Be available to listen to families in transition.* For example, visit a family going through a divorce and ask parents to tell you their stories and experiences. Don't judge the situation. Work to understand what's happening so you can better minister to the family.

• *Work with families to develop a theology that fits their family situation, such as a theology of single parenting, a theology of blended families, a theology of adoptive families.* Work together to define a theology that blends Scripture and everyday life.

• *Give support to families who are experiencing any kind of change by introducing them to other families who have gone through the change and are now doing well.* These partnerships give families support and hope.

• *Meet with other church leaders in your area or with family service providers to discuss the types of trends they're seeing in family transitions and crises.* Sometimes it's easy to fall out of the loop with the latest issues and trends facing families, particularly if these families don't attend your church or they keep their pain to themselves.

• *Give all families clear signals about who to call when they're in transition or crisis.* In addition to the name, give the phone number and the times to call. (Often families feel uncomfortable calling a senior minister about a problem or think that their problems are small when compared to a death.) Give families this information *before* they need it.

• *Assign a person to check in periodically with a family going through a transition or crisis.* Most transitions and crises are long-term, and churches can minister more effectively by contacting the family throughout the time of difficulty. The assigned person can make a monthly (or biweekly) note in his or her calendar as a reminder. Continue to check in for at least one year *after* you think the crisis is over since new issues arise during the healing process.

• *Find out about services for families in transition in your community.* Connect with these programs and create ways to serve these families. For example, if you have a place that provides housing for families in transition, perhaps several families in your church can prepare and eat a meal with these families. After the meal, the children can play together while the parents take a short break and get ready for bed.

• *Be intentional about educating members of prayer chains, congregational care leaders, and others who provide support in ways to give support to people in emotional and relationship pain.* (Church people often feel most comfortable giving support to people with physical illnesses.) Work to break through stigmas of divorce, separation, abuse, and other types of emotional and relational pain so that members can provide care instead of judgment.

• *Create a small support group for people in your congregation who are facing a similar crisis.* Consider an unemployment group, a divorce group, a widow/widower's group, or a Chronic Fatigue Syndrome group.

• *Designate a small discretionary fund for your senior pastor who can then give financial aid to families in transition and crisis without committee approval.* These funds are meant to be a one-time gift for the purpose of giving a family a small boost when it is most needed.

Visiting Families

* *Whenever a family joins your church, have a staff person or lay leader visit them at home in order to get to know the family better.*
* *Visit families whenever there's a birth or an adoption of a child.*
* *An ideal time to visit families is during the final two months of pregnancy.* Some churches even create prayer pals who will pray for an expectant mother when she goes into labor and contacts the church office to let people know about the impending birth.
* *Assign each family in your church a new family to shepherd and care for.* Encourage the member family to visit and build relationships with the new family.
* *Make a point of visiting families who have members who don't attend church.* For example, a mother may bring her children to church, but her husband doesn't attend. Visit the entire family at home (when the husband will be there) to get to know the entire family.
* *Consider visiting families during key transitional times, such as a child starting*

CHURCH SPOTLIGHT

offering a Variety of Support Groups

First Baptist Church of Jacksonville, Florida, strengthens families by providing a number of support groups. The church has support groups such as search for significance, breaking the cycle of hurtful family experiences, depression support, cancer support, managing your anger, divorce recovery for kids, and making peace with the past.

MEMORABLE QUOTE

"Family support involves ministering with families in a way that puts them in charge of the care or services they are receiving."

Richard Olson and Joe Leonard, *A New Day for Family Ministry* [7]

kindergarten, a child turning thirteen, a teenager getting a driver's license, a child graduating from high school, a child going to college, and so on. Often these are stressful times for the family.

• *Visit families during the summer.* Although many people go on vacation during the summer, this time of year typically is the most easygoing for families. It's an ideal time of year just to relax and be with families when school and many extracurricular activities aren't in session.

• *Be aware of when family members are having surgery.* Because of the growth of outpatient surgeries, many families don't even tell the church when their children are getting tubes in their ears or having their tonsils removed. Create a climate of caring that says that all surgeries—even outpatient surgeries—are important and are worth a visit either beforehand or after.

• *Visit families who are dealing with chronic illnesses or disabilities.* Often families can become overwhelmed and exhausted by the caregiving and expense that these require. Even though one family member has always used a wheelchair, the family may currently be struggling with a certain aspect of the situation. Periodically check in with families to see how they're doing and what their needs are.

• *The best time to visit a family is for no reason at all.* This demonstrates that you're thinking about the family and want to spend a little time with them.

Support-Group Ideas

• *Create parental support groups according to the age of children in families.* For example, have a group of "Parents of

Toddlers," "Parents of Preschoolers," "Parents of Elementary-Age Children," and "Parents of Teenagers." Even if the groups are small, continue to meet. A support group doesn't need to be large to be effective. In many instances, families want to connect with other families that have children of about the same age, and there are few opportunities to do so.

• *Ask families what types of support groups they would be interested in.* Have an informal "focus group" gathering of a few families to find out what types of support they're interested in. In addition, consider doing a congregational survey to learn about the needs of families.

• *Develop a support group for parents who are parenting alone or are parenting with a nonbelieving (or nonchurchgoing) parent.* Have group members figure out ways to nurture faith in themselves and in their children.

• *Whenever you offer any type of support group for families, always provide a list of reliable referral resources for families who may need more in-depth counseling and therapy.* Some of these resources may be secular, but also check with other churches in your area to find out what resources they have available. One church in your community, for example, may have a Christian counselor as part of its staff.

• *Learn about the various issues families are grappling with and the types of families that are in your congregation.* For example, if your church has several blended families or single-parent families, you could create a support group for those families. Or be aware when similar events happen to families. For example, one church started a support for families experiencing the loss of a loved one when a number of families experienced the death of a family member.

• *If a support group has more than six people present, separate the group into two smaller groups so that everyone gets the chance to talk and share.* If a support group gets too large, people can feel lost and disconnected, particularly if all do not have the opportunity to talk or to fully share their thoughts.

• *Whenever your church offers Bible study groups or other small-group experiences, include at least one group for families.* Schedule the time so that it's easy for families to attend. For example, if you want to create a group for parents, consider offering it during the Christian education hour or other times when parents are bringing their children to church for some type of activity.

CHURCH SPOTLIGHT

Supporting working Parents

Coast Hills Community Church in Aliso Viego, California, an interdenominational church, attracted many new members by offering a number of parent-support groups and classes that gave them information and support. One popular class is "Parenting Before and After Work."

• *Create a support group called "Parents of Faith" for parents interested in learning more about how to be Christian parents.* Have Bible studies about parenting. Talk about how parenting produces both joy and grief by grappling with Proverbs 10:1, 17:25, and 23:24.

• *Create support groups that cater to more general family concerns, rather than just crisis concerns (such as sexual abuse groups, AA groups, and depression groups).* Create support groups such as Christian family finances, Christian family fun, and Christian family faith issues.

• *Look for ways to create support groups, even for small groups of people.* For example, if you have three people in your congregation who are expecting a baby, arrange for a time for them to meet. Even if they never meet again or form an ongoing support group, you have made the first step in creating a caring community for these people within the church.

Chapter 7

Music and the Arts

Creative Activities for families

When churches have family ministries, they often tend not to include music ministries and ministries within the arts. An unspoken assumption exists that if a family happens to be musical, the parents will eventually find the church choir and the children will discover the children's choir. Yet are we overlooking a crucial aspect of family ministry by not including music and the arts? Are we leaving some families' creative abilities untapped?

Even if a family claims that it's not musical, ask family members how many music compact discs, audiotapes, or records they have. Find out how many hours a day family members spend listening to the stereo, the radio, or to some other form of music. More often than not, you'll find that music and the arts are central to the day-to-day activities of most families.

Since music and the arts are such integral parts of church life, how can you bring families and the creative arts at your church together? How can families participate in the creative aspects of worship

CHURCH SPOTLIGHT

A flute choir

Myers Park United Methodist Church in Charlotte, North Carolina, offers a flute choir for anyone who has a basic reading and playing skill of the flute (including children and teenagers learning the instrument).

other than just singing songs and hymns? How can families use their creativity in Christian education classes? How can family members help make artistic decorations and participate in developing the program of a church special event? With the arts and music being so important to families and to churches, why not find out how the two can better intersect?

Engaging families through music and the arts is another way of connecting families to your church as well as to their faith journey. For many families, music and the arts are part of their soul, even if family members don't quite articulate it in that way. Music and the arts have a way of getting under people's skin and tapping their heart in quicker and deeper ways than the spoken word. The arts, including music, are powerful ways to reach and keep families involved in your church.

Vocal Music Ideas

• *Periodically have a song or hymn sing during part of your worship service.* Encourage family members to call out names or numbers of the songs they would like to sing. Be intentional about having children and teenagers give suggestions.

• *Encourage families to sing together and perform together.* Sometimes a family will create a small vocal group (and even learn a two-, three-, or four-part harmony song) to share during a worship service, or two or three family members will sing a duet or trio together. Families don't have to be extremely musical to do this. Sometimes a family with young children can just get up and sing "Jesus Loves Me" together, with everyone singing the melody.

• *Create a family choir that practices and performs periodically.* This group could practice once a month and perform at a worship service three to four times a year.

• *Encourage teenagers who enjoy vocal music at their school to be soloists at your church.* Find out if another family member can accompany the singer with a piano, guitar, or other musical instrument.

• *Create a repertoire of favorite songs and hymns that you sing often in your church.* Once families begin to master these, gradually add a new song or hymn for them to learn. Too often, families end up not learning any church music because few songs and hymns are repeated.

• *Periodically have the children's music director or leader teach families in worship simple songs of faith that also include hand motions or actions.* Encourage families to learn these selections by providing the music and words for them to take home with them.

• *The season of the church year in which families tend to know the most songs is Advent and Christmas.* Be intentional about teaching families songs around Easter, Epiphany, Pentecost, and other church seasons.

• *Ask families to invite extended family members to sing a faith song or hymn that has been a family favorite for a number of generations.*

• *Create an annual family church concert.* This yearly event could be something that families look forward to that doesn't require much preparation time. Or consider having a family church musical. Find music that appeals to children, teenagers, and adults.

• *If your church has only one choir of adults, occasionally invite the children and teenagers of the choir members to sit with the choir and join in during one simple song.* Children often think it's a thrill to sit up in the choir loft, the balcony, or in front of the church with the choir.

• *Consider having your family choir go on tour occasionally.* Few churches have family choirs, and many would welcome the music of your family choir. In addition, families may enjoy singing in other sanctuaries. If you don't have a family choir, consider having a children's choir perform for another church in your community. Families often enjoy seeing other people they know who attend other churches.

• *If your church has singing liturgy, occasionally ask one of your families to lead this part of your worship service.*

• *Create a list of vocal instructors who attend your church.* Make this list available to families who may be interested in taking vocal lessons. If you don't have anyone who teaches voice, find out which teachers are used by members of your congregation who take voice lessons.

• Ask families who enjoy singing to make lullaby musical tapes for families in your church who are expecting or who have infants. Or have the well-known soloist in your church do this for families in your church.

Instrumental Music Ideas

• Create a family music night during which you put together a program of different church families performing in different ways. One family may sing accompanied by a guitar. Another family may play kazoos. Another family may have two members who can play a piano duet.

• Have an intergenerational congregational band that rehearses once a month and performs three to four times a year for worship services and/or other church events. Include children from fifth grade and older in addition to adults of all ages. Encourage musical families to participate together.

• Seek out professional family groups and invite them to perform a concert at your church or during your worship

MORE INFO

Creative Ideas in the Arts

Praising God Through the Lively Arts by Linda M. Goens (Nashville: Abingdon Press, 1999) gives easy-to-use ideas for including the creative arts (such as clowning, liturgical dance, and choral Scripture reading) in worship services.

service. These families may be role models for other families in your church.

• *Encourage families to present special music for worship services, in which even the youngest musicians can participate.* For example, a sixth grader could play a viola solo accompanied by his or her mom. Or a family with young children could bring triangles, tambourines, and wood blocks and perform a simple song.

• *If your church has a church choir that gives a concert or does a music-only worship service occasionally, encourage the music coordinator to also include instrumentalists as part of the program.* Encourage families with children of all ages to participate in this.

• *Offer piano and other individual music lessons at your church during the time that you want parents involved in committee meetings and other church activities.* That way parents can bring their children to weekly music lessons while they participate in other church work.

• *Create a contact list of instrumentalists in your church and distribute this list to families.* Sometimes one family member plays an instrument while others don't, and they're looking for other musicians to work with. For example, you may find three people, one who plays flute, another who plays violin, and another who plays piano who come together to play Brandenburg concertos during your worship. Your music minister or coordinator may also have additional ideas of music that could be performed in your church.

• *If you have a bell choir or some other instrumental choir, look for simple music to provide to families with children.* Encourage parents who play these instruments to play them with their children and occasionally perform these easier pieces.

• *Create music mentors in your church by connecting children and teenagers who play a certain instrument (such as a French horn) with an adult who plays the same instrument.* Music mentors often help families locate other families in your church.

• *If your church has an organ, find out if the organist is willing to give organ lessons to interested family members.*

• *Encourage music teachers in your community to rent your sanctuary for recitals and concerts.* Often music teachers want to have recitals but don't have the space to do so. Announce these recitals and concerts to members of your church.

• *Find children and teenagers who play the piano to perform piano duets for your worship service or other special church activity.*

Ideas in the Arts

• *If you have people who make banners for your church sanctuary, ask them to lead a banner-making class for families.* Families often enjoy making church banners together, particularly when they can learn from other people who have experience.

• *Invite a stained-glass artist to offer a class showing families how to*

BONUS IDEA

Making Music During Worship

Create musical readings and liturgies in which family members can participate by playing simple instruments (such as sand blocks, sticks, triangles, and so on) to scriptures about music, such as Nehemiah 12:27-30, Psalm 98, Psalm 150, Daniel 3:8-18, and 1 Corinthians 14:7-12. Or create readings and liturgies where family members clap, stomp their feet, whistle, and make other musical sounds without instruments.

make stained art. Many church-going families enjoy stained glass, but it's often difficult for them to find people who teach the art.

• *If your church has many families who enjoy making things together, have an annual arts fair where families can display their projects and sell them.*

• *Occasionally have a family craft-making event at your church where families can pick from three or four (or more) art stations.* Set up art stations that aren't typical, such as making piñatas, plaster of Paris masks, or plaster of Paris biblical maps.

• *Create family craft activities that tie into the church year.* Design Ukrainian Easter eggs near the end of Lent. Make Christian symbol ornaments during Advent.

• *Find families who enjoy floral arranging.* Ask them to make floral arrangements for your altar to display for a worship service or a special event.

• *Have families make Advent wreaths.* You can find instructions for making grapevine wreaths, straw wreaths, or Styrofoam rings in many Christian holiday books. Or have families make advent Yule logs.

Help families identify stores where they can purchase purple and pink advent candles, or buy them in bulk and have them available for families to purchase from your church.

• *During Advent, have a gift-making workshop for families to come and make gifts for friends and family.* Have crafts that families can do together and also ones for children to work on separately to make a surprise gift (that they also wrap) to put under the tree. Most families are happy to pay craft and art materials fees. Find people in your church who have creative fingers to lead the different gift-making stations.

• *Create a series of art-making activities during Advent, Lent, or other times of the church year.* Two helpful resources (full of creative crafts for families) are: *Before and After Easter: Activities and Ideas for Lent to Pentecost* by Debbie Trafton O'Neal (Minneapolis: Augsburg Fortress, 2001) and *Before and After Christmas: Activities for Advent and Epiphany* by Debbie Trafton O'Neal (Minneapolis: Augsburg Fortress, 1991). The author's crown of thorns wreath on page 6 of *Before and After Easter* is especially creative and can offer families a way to mark Lent and the days of Holy Week.

• *Ask families to design the front cover of your church bulletin or your church newsletter from time to time.* Or ask families to contribute artwork to place throughout the bulletin or newsletter.

• *Have an annual church art fair where you display works of art made by family members throughout your church.* If you have many people who want to do this, consider having an art month

MORE INFO

Music Ministry Ideas

100 Ideas for Music Ministry compiled by Mark Cabaniss and Phil Mitchell (Milwaukee: Hal Leonard, 1998) tells how to build a stronger music ministry through this book and audiocassette package.

during which a number of artists are each assigned one to two weeks to display their art.

• *Hold a creative arts event during the summer for families with infants, toddlers, and preschoolers.* On a sunny day, give young children new paintbrushes and squirt bottles to create temporary works of art by using water (not paint). Children can paint on sidewalks, walls, and other outdoor canvases. They can delight in their creations and marvel at how slowly or quickly these creations disappear.

• *Update the art materials in Christian education classrooms, family education classrooms, and arts and crafts centers periodically throughout the year.* Many churches use their entire art supply budget once a year (typically in September). By January, most of these materials are well used or used up.

• *Sponsor an outdoor art fair at your church during the summer.* Set up arts and crafts booths for family members to do art projects. Hang rope, string, or yarn between trees and pillars so that works of art can be displayed by being hung by clothespins.

Ideas in Creative Movement and Drama

• *Create simple creative movements for one to three families to do as a processional for a worship service.* In a single line, family members can take three steps forward, one step back, pause for one beat and then repeat the process again. Each family member carries a significant worship item, such as offering plates before or after an offering, items for Communion, items for baptism, the Bible, or something else.

• *Find out if any families know clowning or miming that they can do for worship or other church events.* Or consider having an expert come to teach family members how to do clowning. Two helpful resources are: *Clown Ministry* by Floyd Shaffer and Penne Sewall (Loveland, Colo.: Group Books, 1984) and *Clown Ministry Skits for All Seasons* (Loveland, Colo.: Group Books, 1990).

• *See if any families know puppeteering and invite them to share their talents.* For example, one parent may be a ventriloquist with a special puppet that could visit your worship service for a children's sermon periodically. Or a family could put on a short puppet skit to a Christian message that fits your worship theme.

• *Occasionally encourage families to stand and do simple movements to hymns and songs.* For example, families could sway to the beat and then hold hands as you end the song with an "Amen." One Chicago congregation closes with the first verse of the hymn "Blest Be the Tie That Binds" every Sunday as a benediction, and everyone in the congregation moves to ensure they're holding hands with someone else

MEMORABLE QUOTE

"People are looking for preaching, music, and liturgy that connect with their everyday lives."

Craig Mueller, pastor of Holy Trinity Lutheran, Chicago, Illinois[3]

CHURCH SPOTLIGHT

Linking Music Mentors with Families

First Presbyterian Church in Knoxville, Tennessee, uses its church during the underutilized daytime hours to provide music lessons for children and families who otherwise could not afford them. "We realized that while it's normal for those of us with middle-class backgrounds to have grown up with piano lessons or dance lessons, it's not for others," says the teacher who helped start the program in the

(continued on next page)

so that everyone in worship is connected.

• *Find out if any families are taking dance lessons.* If so, ask family members to lead the congregation in a meditation or prayer through a short dance piece.

• *Include family members as part of readings or skits.* For example, during Advent, have a pregnant mother read Mary's song of praise (Luke 1:46-55). Have a family with many young children read the passage of Jesus blessing the children (Matthew 19:13-15, Mark 10:13-16, or Luke 18:15-17) with the parents standing alone at first and then the children gradually running up to join the parents by the end of the reading.

• *Create prayers, meditations, and liturgies that have family members doing motions with their hands,* such as reaching up toward the heavens, reaching out to each other, hugging themselves, folding into prayer, and opening up to give.

• *See if any families are gymnasts, and have family members create a short gymnastic routine (with cartwheels, somersaults, and hand stands) to a liturgical reading or meditation.*

• *Find out if anyone knows sign language.* Have that person teach families a short prayer in sign language that becomes a regular part of your worship.

• After you baptize or dedicate a baby, carry the child with you as you walk throughout the congregation, introducing the child to everyone and everyone to the child.

Ideas in Writing and Literature

• Invite families to contribute short devotions to create a short family devotional for Advent or Lent. If you'd like, encourage a theme for families to write about. Encourage families to submit their favorite poems, original writings, scripture passages, and family stories. Then put these together into a short devotional booklet to distribute to families.

• Ask families to name their favorite Christian books. Create a book list of favorites. Divide books by category: parenting, picture books, books for elementary-age children, books for teenagers, novels, memoirs, devotional books, and so on.

• Find out about the writing interests of families. For example, you may discover a number of family members interested in writing memoirs, poetry, short stories, or genealogical stories. Create a group that meets monthly to write together and talk about their writing process.

Church Spotlight
(continued)

downtown church. Music teachers (both from within and outside the congregation) were recruited to teach the lessons. Church leaders then raised funds for the teachers and the musical instruments from many community sources, such as the Knoxville Housing Authority, the Junior League, the Knoxville Arts Alliance, and the Knoxville Parks and Recreation Department. About forty children and youth take music lessons. In addition, each is paired with an adult artist/mentor from the community.

• *Have a poetry workshop or class where you teach family members to write Christian haiku, blank verse, sonnets, free verse, and limericks.* If you find many interested people, consider creating a congregational booklet of poetry.

• *Create family book-reading discussion groups.* Choose books that have Christian themes, such as novels and memoirs by Maya Angelou, Frederick Buechner, Annie Dillard, Madeleine L'Engle, Gail Godwin, Jan Karon, Anne Lamott, C. S. Lewis, and Henri Nouwen.

• *Find a sister congregation in another state, city, or country.* Create family pen pals so that families from your church can write to families from your sister congregation.

• *Bring families together who enjoy creating baby books, creative memory scrapbooks, photo albums, or other types of records of family life.* Encourage family members to work together on these and to get to know each other as they work. Children and teenagers often enjoy putting together scrapbooks and photo albums that record parts of their lives.

• *Start a family journaling group that gets together to talk and journal.* Some churches have created classes based on *The Artist Way: A Spiritual Path to Higher Creativity* by Julia Cameron with Mark Bryan (New York: Jeremy P. Tarcher, 1992).

• *Have a hymn-writing session in your church where you have family members take the tunes of well-known hymns and write new lyrics (words) to them.* Some family members become quite adept at creating new verses for songs and hymns that churches can then use as part of worship. Check copyright rules before printing music.

• *Find the names of all the published authors in your church.* Create a book list of their works. Most churches have a least one author. If your church doesn't have any authors as members, ask if anyone in your congregation has family or friends who are authors.

Chapter 8

Special Activities

With families' jammed-packed schedules, why bother with fun and games for families at church? Because that's what families need.

"Half the population now says they have too little time for their families," says Juliet B. Schor, Ph.D., author of *The Overworked American: The Unexpected Decline of Leisure*.[1] Churches that provide relaxing, fun ways for families to be together are providing a ministry that few families receive.

Creating special church activities for families helps to:

• *Make families more comfortable with coming to church: a number of families feel somewhat awkward in church.* Many parents are newcomers to church, even if they grew up in the church. A large segment of parents who dropped out of church after confirmation or high school are returning after they have children. Because of this, they're somewhat familiar with the church; but they're also uneasy. Creating special activities at the church (or connected with the church) that don't seem overly religious can often help families feel comfortable about coming to church on a more regular basis. Special activities give families the chance to better know

FAST FACT

Longing for
Time Together

In a survey of 1,200 five- to
sixteen-year-olds, 76 percent
said they wanted to spend more
time with their parents.[2]

the church —and other families—on a more informal basis. These types of activities help families become more at ease with being church members again.

• *Cement relationships between family members: family members who play together are more apt to stay together.* In our current society, so much of play promotes isolation instead of community. Children play individual handheld games. Family members play games on the computer (individually, of course). Children and teenagers play sports—but on teams that are age segregated, such as the high school basketball team or the third-grade soccer team. Very few families experience any type of play activity together. Watching television together doesn't count. It doesn't build any sense of community. Providing special activities for families to do together at church can bring families closer and teach family members new ways to "hang out" with each other.

• *Open up families: When families are at a church overnight or flying kites at church, they're more apt to talk to each other.* By building in conversation starters with an event or outing, churches can encourage families to open up. Family members often notice how bowling as a family on a church bowling night brings them together.

• *Affirm families: families feel appreciated and affirmed when churches create activities that bring*

families together rather than pull them apart. When churches honor family relationships (such as by having a father-son barbecue or a mother-daughter makeover), families sense that the church values family relationships.

• *Encourage families to stretch further: many families have wounds that are not talked about or addressed.* When families start spending time together and begin to have more trust in each other, issues that need to be addressed often start coming to the surface. It's harder for children to say, "I'm really lonely, and I want some of your time," when family members are going in fifteen different directions all at once. Children are more apt to say, "I wish you spent more time with me" when families start spending time together.

• *Build family spirituality: "Play is a child's prayer.* For a child, to play is to pray. True child's play opens the door to a life of true prayer," writes Jean Grasso Fitzpatrick in her book *Something More: Nurturing Your Child's Spiritual Growth.* "Prayer as play may sound like a revolutionary idea, but it has long been recognized as such in various religious traditions. To set aside 'productive' work and leave room in the week for 'useless' activities that seem to open us up to the sacred: this has always been the gift of the Sabbath."[3] Special activities can help families grow deeper in faith because these activities build relationships and help family members start talking.

Planned fun and games at church often have a very serious side to them. Those doing the planning know that these activities attract many more families since the activities don't seem overly religious. They know that families need time to just play and hang out together. They know that giving families opportunities to be together is an essential part of your family ministry.

Honoring Family Relationships

• *Have a mother-son milk and cookies gathering for families with children.* Or have a mother-son event for families with teenagers where the sons take their mothers on a date. Celebrate the relationship of mothers and sons.

• *Create stickers, bumper stickers, buttons, T-shirts, tote bags, or pens that show your church's commitments to families.* For example, consider slogans such as, "Families First at UMC" or "Families Together at First Lutheran" or "Caring Families at St. Mark's."

• *Organize a guy's night out for dads and sons.* Have a barbecue, cookout, or a pizza party, for example. Talk about the importance of dads and sons spending time together to form strong relationships.

• *Have an event that recognizes the relationship between siblings.* Talk about their important role, how to live together, how to negotiate conflict, and how to show your appreciation for each other.

• *Honor the relationships between fathers and daughters by having a father-daughter iced tea.* Serve cake and iced tea. Have someone give a short message about the remarkable relationships between dads and daughters.

• *Celebrate family week during the first week of May,* which is when many Christian churches celebrate families. Encourage families to wear similar clothes (such as red shirts and jeans). Emphasize the importance of families sticking together through both easy and difficult times. Make a small ribbon, badge, button, or sticker that has a positive message about families for each family member to wear.

• *Have a mother-daughter makeover* where moms and daughters come together to deepen their relationship. After a fun activity (such as a hike, picnic, pool party, or cookout), talk about how to make the mother-daughter bond even better. Tie in the scripture 2 Corinthians 5:17-21 and talk about how we can become new creations. Discuss the differences between "looking" like new creations and "acting" like new creations.

• *Have families recognize National Grandparents Day on the first Sunday after Labor Day.* Create projects that families could make for grandparents, such as recording an audiotape of memories, shooting a videotape of songs and stories, or making a family favorites book with stories, recipes, jokes, and family sayings.

• *Pay attention to the types of families you have in your church.* How can you link families together that honors their family type? For example, one church created a group for families with adopted children because of the number of adoptive families in the church. In another church, a group was formed by gathering families with only one child.

MORE INFO

family fun and Games

New Games for the Family by Dale N. LeFevre (New York: Perigee Books, 1988) includes a large number of creative ways for families to play together and have fun.

• *Celebrate extended family connections* by coming together and taking multigeneration pictures of each other (for families with extended family members nearby) and writing cards to send to those who live far away.

Family Fellowship Activities

• *Find out the day your church was begun and throw an annual "Congregational Family Birthday" party.* Have a cake with the correct number of candles. (Get a staff person, a lay minister, one family with children, and one single older adult to blow out the candles together.) Decorate your church, sing "Happy Birthday" to your church, and enjoy the party.

• *Create a fellowship activity based on bingo, except create a card with six boxes across and six boxes down (for a total of 36 boxes).* Spell the word FAMILY at the top with each letter of the six-letter word representing one of the six columns. Create 36 different categories for each of the 36 boxes. Categories could include: *Been a member at this church for at least ten years; Have two children; Live in an apartment; A family member plays on a sports team; Are a new member of the church; Have grandparents who live close by; A family member plays a musical instrument, and so on.* When families arrive, give each family one FAMILY card. Have families stick together and meet other families. When a family fits the description of a box, that family writes the family name in the box. The first family to get either six across, six down, or six diagonally (from either the top left-hand side or the top right-hand side) is the winner.

• *Have a family breakfast to meet the church staff one Saturday morning.* Serve muffins and fruit. Make sure all your church staff and key lay leaders come to eat breakfast with families. Allow time for families to ask church staff questions. Some churches have had an "Eat and Talk with the Senior Pastor Breakfast."

• *Have families create a collage about their family* that includes photos of their families, favorite sayings, humorous incidents, and family favorites. Have families post these collages in one area of your church. Then have families get together to see each other's collages and talk with each other.

• *Have a family ice-cream social during the summer or a hot chocolate and cookies social during the winter.*

• *Create a families first event.* Have families come together and form small groups (but keep families together). Have family members talk about these family firsts: *their first memory of their family, their first major vacation, their first big disagreement and what it was about, their first humorous family incident, their first family faith experience, their first family pet, their first family home, their first family church.*

• *Have families come together and make family crafts.* Choose crafts that are interesting and new to parents but also ones that allow families to talk with each other during the creation.

• Whenever you're serving a meal for a fellowship activity, *create simple place mats with discussion questions written on them.* Choose questions that

MEMORABLE QUOTE

"By permitting yourself to indulge in a good time and rekindle nostalgic feelings of childhood, you soothe your body as well as your soul."

Alix Strauss, freelance writer[4]

will help people talk to each other more easily and get to know each other.

• *Have a family car show-and-tell.* During the summer, have families bring their cars to the church parking lot and park them for show. Have families open up the trunks and car doors so that other families can see inside. (Encourage families to bring in their cars without changing anything about them.) Families often get a big chuckle to see how other families have stuffed trunks or have three car seats lined up in the backseat with Cheerios and animal cracker crumbs all over the floor.

• *Early in the Advent season have a family cookie exchange.* Have each family make four to six dozen of their favorite Christmas cookies to bring to exchange with other families. (It's much easier for families to make four to six dozen of one kind of cookie than to make four to six different kinds of cookies.) Children and teenagers especially like this type of activity.

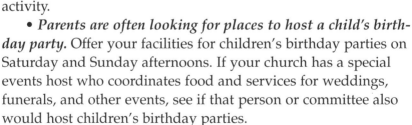

• *Parents are often looking for places to host a child's birthday party.* Offer your facilities for children's birthday parties on Saturday and Sunday afternoons. If your church has a special events host who coordinates food and services for weddings, funerals, and other events, see if that person or committee also would host children's birthday parties.

• *Have families each bring in one object that symbolizes their family.* For example, a family could bring in a portable tape-recorder and push fast forward and say that the family always feels like it's moving in fast forward. Another family may bring in a rock to symbolize how solid the family is. Another family could bring in crazy glasses that have a mustache and a large nose and talk about the family's sense of humor. Have families take turns telling about their symbols.

• *Host a family progressive dinner for your church.* Once interested families sign up, create groups of five families. (Ideally, create family groups according to similar ages of children.) Have the first three groups make appetizers and the last two groups make desserts. (That way no one has to have the expense of putting on the main course.) Create the order of the family homes to visit (from first to fifth) and the time frame. Have family groups meet at the first house and have the appetizer before moving to the second home. Progressive dinners are often good ways for families to get to know each other and to visit one another's homes.

• *Have a family collections gathering.* Encourage family members to bring a part of their collection to show to other families. (Encourage each family member to bring in part of a collection, not just the children.) Have families display their collections near each other. Have family members take turns telling the group about their collections so that people can connect which collections belong to which family.

• *Have families meet after a worship service at a local restaurant or fast-food place to fellowship and be together.* Since many families are very busy, they tend not to come to potluck gatherings that require bringing a dish prepared to share.

• *After any kind of church gathering (such as a worship service or a family ministry event), have coffee, water, and juice available* (and possibly cookies or something simple to eat) to encourage families to stay and socialize with one another.

Sports and Recreation Activities

• *Have families with teenagers go on a church golf outing.* Or consider having families with children of all ages play miniature golf together.

• *In the summer, have your "Mom's Day Out" meet at a local playground* where moms can play with their children and also talk with other moms.

• *Organize a family kick ball game* so families with preschoolers, elementary-age children, and teenagers can all participate.

• *Have a "Bible Study and Bowl"* event where families gather for a family Bible study at the church and then go bowling afterward.

• *If your church has a gym or outdoor basketball court, have a family basketball game.* Have children play against parents, who must play in pairs with one of their legs tied to a partner. Make ties from ripped-up old sheets.

• *Have a sand-castle building event at a nearby beach.* Talk about Matthew 7:24-27.

• During times of the year when weather can drive people indoors, *have a family fun night where families come together and play board games.* Many board games can have up to fourteen players, and many families are used to playing with only two to three players.

• *Have a family bingo night.* Children enjoy playing this game with their parents and other families. Children enjoy the event even more when there are prizes to be won.

• *Host a family ball bonanza.* Invite families to your church yard, park, or gymnasium to have a "ball." Plan different activities that families can do with balls, such as learn to juggle, do bouncing ball relays, or sit on the floor and roll balls back and forth to toddlers and preschoolers.

• *Have a penny hunt on your church grounds for families.* See which families can find the most pennies. Have families guess how many pennies were hidden and how many will remain lost after the event. Tie in to the parable of the lost coin in Luke 15:8-10.

• *Organize a family hike.* Ideally find a location that has easy, short trails for families with young children and a location that also has longer, more challenging trails for older children and teenagers. Some churches go to state parks, nature reserves, mountain areas, or the woods.

• *Have a family relay night.* For example, have a snowshoe relay (where team members must slide their feet on 8 1/2 x 11 paper, as if the paper were snowshoes, to the goal and back). Organize a stunt relay where each relay team member is assigned a stunt to perform, such as doing forward somersaults, hopping on one foot, skipping, carrying another team member, and so on.

• *Have a frozen turkey bowling event for families.* Use a frozen turkey as a bowling ball to knock down pins on a gymnasium floor or sidewalk.

• *Have a family treasure hunt at your church.* Have someone at the door to greet families as they arrive and give each family a clue. The first clue says, "Go to the door and go 24. Look in a

BONUS IDEA

Search Through the Church

Have a family scavenger hunt in your church. Get the church staff involved and stationed in different places of your church. When a staff person is found, that staff person signs the scavenger hunt paper that the family has. Include places such as these: the pulpit (the pastor is stationed there), the church

(Continued on next page)

place where you can see your face." The next clue, which is 24 steps away and hanging on the mirror, says, "The next place to look is where church people cook." Hanging on the door to your church kitchen is the next clue, which says, "Someone worked harder than a mouse to care for this church house. Find this man to go on with your plan." Hanging on your church custodian's door is the next clue, which says, "Someone is wearing blue. Find the clue on the bottom of his or her shoe." Have someone completely dressed in blue with the next clue taped on the bottom of his or her shoe, which says, "Your next clue is really good. It's behind something made of wood." Behind a wooden door, have your family ministry gathering or event.

• *Have a "thumbody" family event* where families make thumb print pictures, sing "Where is Thumbkin," have thumb wrestling matches, have short Bible studies where families read about how family members are "thumbody" special, such as Psalm 139:13-15 and Ephesians 1:3-14.

Outdoor Family Activities

• *Have a movie under the stars night for families to watch movies outdoors on warm summer nights.* Show family movies that promote positive values and encourage faith building. Consider having an early showing for families with young children and serving animal crackers and juice. Have a showing after that for children with elementary-age children, and serve popcorn and soda pop. Then have a late showing for families with teenagers.

• *Have Bible stories in the park.* Have families with teenagers act out Bible stories for families with younger children. To add excitement, have the actors create skits from Bible stories for the audience to guess.

• *Have families meet at a community pool or beach and have a family fun time outdoors.* Some churches organize this by having one to two teenagers supervise and play with children while the parents have a Bible study or a community-building activity. Then everyone comes together to play.

• *If your area gets snow, organize a family snow creation activity.* Families can create a crèche out of snow or make caroling snow people near your church entrance.

• *Have families take a trip to a nearby city and take a walking tour of the churches and cathedrals.* If you make arrangements ahead of time, you often can arrange a tour of one or two cathedrals or get permission to explore their sanctuaries.

Bonus Idea
(continued)

office (church secretary or volunteer), the youth group room (youth leader), the Christian education office (Christian education coordinator), the organ/piano (organist/pianist), the broiler room or maintenance area (janitor), the nursery (caregiver), committee meeting room (head lay leader), a children's Sunday school room (a children's Sunday school teacher), an adult education room (an adult education leader), and others in your church. This is a fun way for families to become more familiar with your church facilities and the church leadership.

• *Go on a hike for families to collect leaves, rocks, bird feathers, and/or sticks to use in making a small altar or to fill a basket to display in their homes.* Collecting gifts of nature can remind families to thank God for creation and the world's abundance.

• *Organize a family fishing outing.* As you fish, talk about the scripture tie-ins to fishing, such as: Ezekiel 47:8-12, Amos 4:1-3, Matthew 13:47-50, Mark 1:14-20, Luke 5:1-11.

• *Organize a family stroller, wagon, tricycle, bicycle ride.* Families on bicycles will take the lead and go on a much longer ride while families with strollers, wagons, and tricycles will enjoy a shorter, more leisurely ride.

• *Consider an outdoor family fair.* The youth group could set up face painting and have games to play. Older adults could have food available. Someone who enjoys photography could take pictures. Musicians could perform. A Christian parenting author could be the invited speaker.

Family Camps, Retreats, and Overnight Ideas

• *Have a family camp-in or camp-out at your church.* Have families bring sleeping bags and pup tents to sleep in your church gym or fellowship center (if you want to have a camp-in) or set up a campsite outside on your church grounds. Who says you need to travel far to have a family camp-out?

• *Check with your church's denominational office to find out about family camps in your area.* If your denomination doesn't offer camps, check with your state's church council. A number of Christian campgrounds now offer week-long or weekend family camps. If you have trouble locating a Christian family camp, have your church reserve a campground for a week and create your own family camp.

• *Have family overnight at your church emphasizing spiritual growth in families.* Have family members bring sleeping bags. Organize family Bible studies, family sing-a-long times, family recreational activities, a family worship service, and family crafts. Because of busy family schedules, consider starting the overnight at dinner time on a Friday night and ending with lunch on Saturday. Charge a nominal fee to cover the cost of food and materials.

• To meet the needs of families as a group as well as individual family members, *have a family overnight or retreat where part of the time you encourage families' spiritual growth as a family and part of the time you separate parents from children.* During those times, have one leader work with parents about Christian parenting issues and another leader work with children about being Christian children or getting along as siblings.

MORE INFO

Inexpensive Ideas for Families

Affordable Family Fun, by Susan L. Lingo (Loveland, Colo.: Group Books, 1997) gives parents and church leaders fun, easy ways to get families of four- to twelve-year-olds playing, talking, and laughing together. Each activity includes a Bible tie-in.

• *Develop an overnight outing or retreat called "Christian Family Fun."* Teach families how to have wholesome Christian family fun that brings family members together and creates a sense of joy and laughter.

• *Create a family getaway that teaches families practical spiritual disciplines,* such as family prayers, family meditations, family Bible studies, family worship, family devotions, and family service. Don't assume that families know how to do the basics, so start with the basics and go deeper from there.

CHURCH SPOTLIGHT

Colorful Skies

Christ Lutheran Church in Fairfax, Virginia, encourages families and people of all ages to spend a morning flying kites in the park. Each spring the church hosts this event to encourage families and people of all ages to mix and mingle with one another.

• *To encourage marriages to flourish, a number of churches offer marriage encounter weekend getaways for couples.* A number of denominations have created their own marriage encounter weekends, such as the United Methodist Marriage Encounter (www.encounter.org), the Episcopal Marriage Encounter (www.episcopalme.com), and the International Lutheran Marriage Encounter (www.ilme.org). In addition, the National Marriage Encounter (1-800-828-3351; www.marriage-encounter.org) can also connect you with Christian marriage encounter retreats in your area.

• *Have a family overnight event during which you encourage families to get into small groups and talk about meaningful family faith stories.* Encourage families to talk about their ancestors' faith stories, and also favorite scriptures and why these scriptures were important.

• *Encourage small groups of families from your church to take a weekend or week-long getaway together.* For example, four or five families could rent a bank of cabins at a resort on a lake, or a number of families could rent a group of rooms at a hotel. Families can play together, eat together, swim, and pray together.

• *Organize a family service overnight.* Start with a family service project Friday evening, have families spend the night in your church, and then finish the service project (or do another) on Saturday morning.

Chapter 9

Take-Home Activities

Nurturing Faith at Home

Families will not go far if the only time they examine faith issues is when they come to church. Families who are faithful in coming each Sunday and don't talk about faith issues at all the rest of the week are like families who eat a balanced, nutritious meal once a week and then devour junk food—or no food at all—the rest of the week. This practice will not sustain them.

Yet how often do we help families integrate faith into their daily lives? How often do we give them take-home faith activities to use from Monday through Saturday? Many churches offer daily devotionals for families, but how many families actually use them? How many have tried to use them and have found they do not fit with the issues they're dealing with?

Nurturing the faith of family members at home isn't an easy task. There's often so much that remains unseen—until years later. Yet, many of our present Christian role models (people such as former president Jimmy Carter, Children's Defense Fund president Marian Wright Edelman, social activist Jim Wallis, Habitat for Humanity founder Millard Fuller, writer Madeleine L'Engle, community organizer Eugene Rivers, and writer Mary Gordon) talk not only about the central focus the church had in their childhood but also about the everyday way faith permeated their lives.

"The legacies that parents and church and teachers left to my generation of Black children were priceless but not material: a living faith reflected in daily service, the discipline of hard work and stick-to-it-ness, and a capacity to struggle in the face of adversity. Giving up and 'burnout' were not part of the language of my elders—you got up every morning and you did what you had to do and you got up every time you fell down and tried as many times as you had to to get it done right. They had grit. They valued family life, family rituals, and tried to be and to expose us to good role models." Marian Wright Edelman writes in *The Measure of Our Success*.[1] "I have always believed that I could help change the world because I have been lucky to have adults around me who did—in small and large ways."[2]

Years ago the extended family was close by; family rituals were more clear; and the church the family attended was often the same place that parents, grandparents, and great grandparents went. Families now often attend a church that no other family members attend (and often is of a different denomination or faith tradition). Extended family lives far away, and sometimes doesn't

FAST FACT

Talk at Home About Faith

In a survey of Christian adults and young people, researchers found that most families talk about faith when children are young. In a survey of adults, 26 percent said they never or rarely talked to their mothers about faith or God when they were between the ages of five and twelve. By the time they were thirteen to eighteen, 58 percent said they never or rarely talked to their dads about faith or God and 51 percent never or rarely

(Continued on next page)

have much contact with family members. Many families are discarding traditional family rituals because they no longer fit, are too painful, or no longer have meaning for them. Unfortunately, few families are replacing discarded rituals with more meaningful traditions.

That's why churches that want to nurture faith in families have a unique—yet critical—opportunity to help families see how faith plays an important role in all of life—including life at home. "The family is the most significant place where faith development occurs," says the congregational ministries coordinator at Trinity Lutheran in Stillwater, Minnesota. "We are intentional about making families faith-forming centers. It is hard to hear about grace, forgiveness, and unconditional love one hour a week and understand those concepts—if they are not practiced and discussed at home. We try to build up the family as the 'first church,' the congregation as the second."[4]

Building each family as the first church entails creating ways to talk about faith that all family members understand. It's about teaching families how to pray and how to find

fast fact (continued)

talked to other relatives about this issue.

What adults remember about their childhood mirrors what young people currently experience. While 38 percent of sixteen- to eighteen-year-olds said they never or rarely talked to their mothers about faith issues between the ages of five to twelve, 56 percent said they never or rarely talked to their fathers about faith or God between the ages of thirteen and fifteen.[3]

family religious rituals that have meaning and significance. Getting started in this area may mean scouring the shelves at Christian bookstores. However, be mindful that the theology of many Christian resources for families may differ from yours. Therefore, it's essential to spend time reading through any published books, pamphlets, or periodicals before giving anything to families.

In addition to reviewing existing material, many churches have started developing their own resources. Some publish their own devotional booklets for families. Others adapt or create new religious rituals for families. Still others create workshops and classes to teach families about how to nurture faith in their home. The important thing is simply to start in some way. "Spiritual nurture begins with the everyday care we give our children," writes Jean Grasso Fitzpatrick in *Something More: Nurturing Your Child's Spiritual Growth*. "It begins when we are ready and willing to explore the rich sources of spirituality that are present in our lives seven days a week."[5] When we give families practical ways to build and nurture faith at home, we help them grow in new ways. We help them see that being Christian means living faith-filled lives every day of the week.

Bible Study Take-Home Ideas

• *Develop a congregational audiocassette that has stories of faith.* Record your church staff and lay leaders each reading a different faith story. Include stories such as Noah and the Ark

(Genesis 6-8), Baby Moses (Exodus 1-2), Crossing the Red Sea (Exodus 13-15), David and Goliath (1 Samuel 17), Daniel and the Lions (Daniel 6), Jonah and the Whale (Jonah 1-4), the Birth of Jesus (Luke 2), the Sermon on the Mount (Matthew 5-7), Jesus Calms the Storm (Mark 4), the Feeding of the 5,000 (John 6), the Good Samaritan (Luke 10), the Crucifixion (Mark 15), and the Resurrection (Mark 16).

• *Read a Bible verse and pray.* Write Bible verses on separate pieces of paper. Place the verses in little boxes and give one to each family. When the family gets together for a meal or a family Bible study, suggest that family members take turns drawing a verse from the box. Read the verse aloud, and then have that person lead the family in prayer.

MORE INFO

fun for families

The Youth & Family Institute of Augsburg College publishes a sixteen-page Faithlife in the Home catalog that has resources for families to nurture faith in their children and teenagers at home. Contact Youth & Family Institute of Augsburg College, Campus Box 70, 2211 Riverside Avenue, Minneapolis, MN 55454-1351; (877) 239-2492; www.youthfamilyinstitute.com.

• *Use a Bible atlas to find the location of Bible stories.* Talk about the setting of the scripture passage.

• *Encourage families to use children's, youth, and illustrated Bibles for family Bible study.* Some churches give children a Bible at specific ages: a preschool Bible at age 3, a children's Bible at second or third grade, a youth Bible at seventh grade, and a study Bible at

CHURCH SPOTLIGHT

Merry christmas Baskets

Families at Pantego Bible Church in Arlington, Texas, can pick up kits to make Merry Christmas Baskets for widows and widowers in their church. The church has a family ministry booth set up in the lobby that is staffed by someone who explains how to make the basket and tells who the recipient will be.

confirmation or high school graduation to encourage the faith development of children and youth as they mature.

• *Place a scripture verse on the bathroom mirror each week.* At mealtime discuss the verse as a family. Have family members memorize it. An option is to place a scripture passage on a slip of paper and tuck it under each family member's plate to find at dinner time. After uncovering the verses, discuss their meaning.

• For families with older children and teenagers, *encourage them to create a Bible study movie review after watching a movie or video together as a family.* This entails identifying the key messages of the film and looking up scripture passages to show whether certain messages were Christian, detailing why or why not. This often can lead to lively discussions for families.

• *Help children learn the books of the Bible.* Have families identify stories as "Matthew stories," "Mark stories," "Luke stories," or "John stories" when they're telling stories from one of the four Gospels to their children. This teaches children that the Bible is filled with many books that have

different names while also making the Bible seem more approach-able because of all its stories.

• *Create a Bible study of numbers.*
Get ten slips of paper. Write the numbers 1 to 10 on the slips, with one number on each paper. Place the slips of paper in a jar. Ask a family member to pull out one piece of paper. Look for a book in the Bible that has the same number of chapters as the number on the slip. (For example, the number 1 means one chapter. That could mean the book of Philemon, 2 John, 3 John, or Jude, which are all one-chapter books of the Bible. If the number three is pulled, consider 2 Thessalonians, Titus, or 2 Peter since those books all have three chapters each.) Choose one book. Then for the next number of days (*one* if the number 1 was pulled or *three* if the number 3 was chosen) read one chapter from that Bible book aloud and talk about it.

Prayers and Devotions Take-Home Ideas

• *Ask families to pray together,* using the prompting words that make up the acronym for PRAY: Praise, Repent, Ask, Yield (listen).

• *Create prayers that rhyme for families with young children.* For example, "Good night, sleep tight, God always keeps you in God's sight. Amen." or "God, we thank you for our day. God, we thank you in every way. Amen."

• *Have a parent start the prayer and each family member add a word or two.* For example, say a thank-you prayer, such as

"That you God for . . . " Each family member then adds one word, such as *food, bunnies, friends, soccer,* or *grandparents.* Or say a prayer of confession, such as "God, I'm sorry that . . . " Each family member then adds something, such as "I yelled." "I got mad at the dog." "I didn't read my Bible today." "I didn't make my bed."

• *Make prayer pillows that have a pocket where Bible verses and prayers for each family member can be placed.* Trinity Lutheran in Stillwater, Minnesota, does this. Children receive a prayer card every Sunday to tuck into the pillow's pocket. This prayer card includes a Bible verse, a written prayer, and space for children to add their prayer concerns.[5]

• *Create a family calendar or date book* that includes the birthdays and anniversaries of each family member and their friends. Besides sending a birthday card or calling to give a birthday greeting, also pray for that person or couple on those days.

• *Develop ways to end prayers in creative ways, especially for families with children.* For example, whisper or shout "Amen" at the end. Clap instead of saying "Amen." Give high fives (slapping another person's hand held up high) while saying "Amen."

• *Do alphabet prayers.* Go around the family and have everyone thank God for something that starts with a different letter of the alphabet, going from A to Z. For families with teenagers, do this backward, from Z to A.

• *As you hear on the news about troubled areas in the world, write the name of the country, region, state, or city.* Place it in a small box. Periodically draw out one name and pray for that area and the people who live there.

• *Encourage parents to say a prayer for each child,* asking God to guide, watch over, and bless the child. Parents might say a quiet prayer when checking on children after each child has fallen asleep (or before awakening each child in the morning).

FAST FACT

A Challenge to Churches

When adults rated the quality of thirty different aspects of congregational life, the one aspect that they rated last was how the congregation helps parents learn how to nurture the faith of their children. Only 20 percent of adults say their churches help them do this.[7]

Advent Take-Home Ideas

• *Give each child a Christian Advent calendar* that starts on the first of December. Find ones with pictures for young children. Some churches even create a family Advent devotional with a short scripture reading, prayer, and short activity for each day (or Sunday) in Advent.

• *Give each family a twelve-inch tapered white candle.* Hand write the numbers 1 through 25 on the candle, starting with 1 near the wick, and ending with 25 near the bottom of the candle. Encourage families to light the candle on the

"It is through our everyday relationship with [our children] that we convey spirituality. As we share our reverence for the natural world, the simple joys of family life, our dependability, and our unconditional love, we show them the face of God."

Jean Grasso Fitzpatrick, *Something More: Nurturing Your Child's Spiritual Growth*[8]

first of December and to burn it to the beginning of number 2. Light the candle each day and burn it to the next number until the family reaches Christmas Day with number 25.

• *Make a Jesse tree based on Isaiah 11:1.* Stick branches from a tree in a pot or jar. Place paper symbols representing Christianity on the branches, such as a cross, a star, an angel, a Bible, and so on.

• *Encourage families to have an Advent wreath or set up a workshop for families to each make one* (see chapter 7). Lighting a candle for each Sunday in Advent is an ideal way for families to keep the season of Advent present in their lives and to encourage family members to talk about the story of preparation and birth in Luke 1–2.

• *Each night at dinner time have families choose a Christmas card from the cards received from friends and loved one.* Pray for the individual or family who sent the card.

• *Have families set up an empty nativity scene somewhere in the house.* Place Mary and Joseph at the far end of the house and have the children move Mary and Joseph closer to the manager each day so that Mary and Joseph make it to the stable by Christmas Eve. Throughout Advent, the children also can move in the shepherds and animals.

Parents keep the baby Jesus hidden until Christmas Eve night. After the children have gone to bed, the parents add baby Jesus to the manger scene.

Christmas Take-Home Ideas

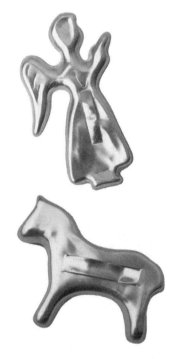

• For families with young children, Christmas Eve can be a long day of waiting. *Create Christmas family activities to do together,* such as making Christmas cut-out sugar cookies of angels, shepherds, sheep, and other nativity scene people and animals. After the cookies have baked, decorate them. On Christmas Eve night, have each family member hold a votive candle. Light each candle one at a time. As each person's candle is lit, have that person tell about what it means that Jesus was born or why he or she is a Christian. After all the candles have been lit and stories told, sing "Silent Night" together. On Christmas Day, read aloud the story of the birth of Jesus in Luke 2.

• *Sing Christmas carols together as a family.* If you have a piano or guitar, have someone play along. If not, sing acappella or sing with a favorite CD. For families who really enjoy music, try to learn harmonies to the carols. Some families go caroling on Christmas Day after all the other festivities have ended.

• After it gets dark, go outside as a family. *Look at the stars* if it isn't cloudy. Find the brightest star. Talk about the Christmas star.

Lent Take-Home Ideas

• *Have families set up seven candles on Ash Wednesday.*
Light the first candle on Ash Wednesday and light one additional
candle each Wednesday. On the Wednesday of Holy Week (which
falls between Palm Sunday and Easter), all candles should be lit.
Light all seven candles again on Maundy Thursday and eat dinner by the candlelight. On Good Friday, turn off all the lights in
the home and light all seven candles. After the candles burn for a
minute or so, extinguish all seven candles so that family members
are sitting in the dark for a few minutes. Then light one candle
and have one family member read aloud Matthew 27:34-54 before
extinguishing the candle.

• *Ask families to each get a flower bulb (such as an amaryllis,
crocus, or hyacinth) at the beginning of Lent.* Throughout the
Lenten season, the bulb will send out a shoot
and usually will bloom toward the end
of Lent. This symbolizes the new life
coming.

• *Have family members wash
one another's feet like Jesus did
in John 13:5-15.* Get a large bowl
and fill it with warm water.
Have a towel nearby and have
family members take turns
washing each other's feet. Each
family member should wash
the feet of one other family
member.

• *Have family members get
Easter baskets with liners and fill
them with dirt.* At the beginning of
Lent, plant grass seed in each basket.
Throughout Lent water the soil. By
Easter, the baskets should be filled with
grass.

Easter Take-Home Ideas

• *Read the Easter story aloud.* Many families read aloud Luke 2 at Christmas time, but few read aloud the Easter story. Start a family tradition of reading aloud different aspects of the Easter story starting on Maundy Thursday. Have family members take turns reading aloud each night with Matthew 26:17-30 on Maundy Thursday, Matthew 27:27-61 on Good Friday, Matthew 27:62-66 on Saturday, and Matthew 28:1-10 on Easter Sunday.

• *Create a family Easter celebration.* Worship services bring out trumpets, lilies, colorful banners, and many other symbols to show the celebratory aspect of Easter. Add symbols of celebration to your Easter family holiday as well, such as having a kazoo march through your backyard (if you have young children) or listening to parts of Handel's *Messiah* (if you have older children). Listen to the *Messiah* pieces in this order: no. 45—Air for Soprano "I Know that My Redeemer Liveth"; no. 46—Chorus "Since by Man Came Death"; no. 47—Recitative for Bass "Behold, I Tell You a

BONUS IDEA

Giving Boxes

Encourage families to place a giving box on their dinner table for family members to place loose change into on a daily basis—even if a family member ends up just giving a penny a day. (Or have a family workshop where families each make a giving box for this.) Having a giving box placed prominently in a place that family members see every day is one way to teach family members the importance of giving.

Mystery"; no. 48—Air for Bass "The Trumpet Shall Sound"; and no. 44—Chorus "Hallelujah!"

• *Have a religious Easter egg hunt.* Consider having two Easter egg hunts: one that has eggs with candy and other treats, and another egg hunt that has eggs with religious symbols inside. Be clear to children which hunt is which so that their expectations are realistic. Hide eggs with Easter symbols, such as nails (John 20:24-29), a stone (Matthew 28:2), an angel (Matthew 28:5-7), a cross (Matthew 27:32), a ripped piece of cloth and/or a broken stone (Matthew 27:51), the number three (Matthew 27:45-50), thorns from a rose bush (Matthew 27:29), a dice (Matthew 27:35), a piece of black construction paper (Matthew 27:45), After children find all the eggs and open them up, have them guess the significance of each item. If they are unsure, have them look up the scripture passage that can give them insight about each symbol.

• *Make plans to plant your Easter lily outside.* Easter lilies will bloom again in September and will come up each spring (even in the coldest of climates) as long as they're planted after the last freeze and are covered up

FAST FACT

Few faith Projects and Devotions

In a survey of sixteen- to eighteen-year-olds involved in a church, 54 percent said they never or rarely had family devotions between the ages of five and twelve, and 64 percent said they never or rarely had family devotions between the ages of thirteen and fifteen.

Families did even worse when it came to doing service and mission projects. Of the same group surveyed, 66 percent said they never or rarely did family projects to help others when they were between the ages of five and twelve. Sixty-three percent said they never or rarely did these types of projects between the ages of thirteen and fifteen.[9]

each winter. Create an Easter lily garden in your backyard or ask your church if your family can create an Easter lily garden on the church grounds.

Other Holiday
Take-Home Ideas

• *For New Year's Day in January*—Read aloud 2 Corinthians 5:17-18. Talk about how each family member can be a "new creation" in the new year.

• *For Candlemas in February*— On February 2nd, light candles to mark the fortieth day after Christmas. It is celebrated as the day that Mary went to temple with baby Jesus to present him. In some Christian traditions, it is also known as the Festival of the Presentation of Christ in the Temple.

• *For Valentine's Day in February*—Cut hearts out of red, white, and pink paper. Write an affectionate, personal note on each valentine and place them around the house for family members to find. Create three to five for each family member. Talk about how God tells us to love one another.

• *For St. Patrick's Day in March*—Reclaim this Christian holiday celebrating St. Patrick of Ireland by looking for three-leaf clovers. Legend says that St. Patrick often used the shamrock as the symbol of the Trinity—the Father, Son, and Holy Spirit. The shamrock shows "three in one and one in three."

MORE INFO

A Christian Family Board Game

The Ungame: Christian Version (available from Cokesbury at 1-800-672-1789; www.cokesbury.com) can be played with two to six family members ages five and up. This noncompetitive game encourages family members to talk about their faith and other issues.

• *For Mother's Day in May*—Plant annuals and perennial flowers in the ground for Mom or Grandma (if she lives in a house) or in pots (if Mom or Grandma lives in a condo, townhouse, or apartment). Spend time together planting.

• *For Father's Day in June*—Make a book titled, "What I Love About Dad" by buying a small photo album (one that holds 12 to 24 photos) and fill it with photographs, drawings, notes, jokes, and memories of Dad.

• *For Independence Day in July*—Highlight similarities between the Israelites becoming free from the Egyptians in the story of the Exodus (Exodus 7) and America becoming independent of English rule. Read aloud the Declaration of Independence. (The encyclopedia has it.) Sing songs such as "God Bless America" and "The Star Spangled Banner." Pray for the leaders of our country and for all the world leaders.

• *For back-to-school days in September*—Write a message in chalk on the sidewalk (if you live in a house) or post a sign that says: Best Wishes Fifth Grader (or whatever grade your child is starting). Take pictures on the first day of school. Send a special treat for the first day of school. Talk about how important education is.

• *For Halloween in October*—Encourage families to do activities that also encourage children to give, rather than just receive. Some churches give children UNICEF Halloween boxes where children also ask for coin donations when they go trick or treating. The Sunday following Halloween, children process forward during worship to place the UNICEF boxes on the altar. Other churches encourage children to give a percentage of their Halloween candy (such as 10 percent or a third) to a food-shelf Halloween box in the church narthex. Although Halloween candy isn't nutritious, all families—even those that use food banks—enjoy candy from time to time. Contact UNICEF, 3 United Nations Plaza, New York, NY 10017; (212)-326-7000; www. unicef.org for boxes.

• *For All Saints Day in November*—Highlight pictures of family members who have died. Talk about their life stories and faith stories. Say a prayer of thanks for their lives.

• *For Thanksgiving in November*—Cut leaf shapes out of red, yellow, orange, and green construction paper. Have family members each

MEMORABLE QUOTE

"Family life is sacred and family activities are holy."

Leif Kehrwald
and Rene Kehrwald,
Families Nurturing Faith[10]

CHURCH SPOTLIGHT

Family Service Project

Families at Salem United Methodist Church in Pocomoke City, Maryland, got together to make dolls for children at the Red Bird Mission in Kentucky. Families (including women, men, and children as young as five years old) got together once a month at the church or in their homes to make fifty dolls. Family members painted faces, sewed dresses, and named each doll. As each doll was completed, it was displayed in the church for members to see. The project caught on throughout the church so that teenagers created doll sponsorships to raise money to go on a mission trip. By the end of the year, the families had made sixty-nine dolls—nineteen more than they had planned to make.

write one thing they're thankful for on a leaf. Create a leaf display on a table or bring in a few branches, place them in a flower vase or jar, and hang leaves from the branches. Use this as a centerpiece for your Thanksgiving table.

Stewardship Take-Home Ideas

• If your church doesn't do so already, *have offering envelopes for children and teenagers.* During worship services, encourage each member of every family (including children and teenagers) to place an offering envelope in the offering plate. This tends to work better during a worship service rather than Christian education hours when children sometimes feel stigmatized for either bringing—or not bringing—an offering. Or if your church wants each family to have only one offering envelope, encourage parents to have their children take turns placing the offering into the offering plate.

• *Have families create a "Lenten box" and place a coin in it each day during Lent.* Each year, encourage families to give more than they did the year before.

• Emphasize to families that stewardship is also about how family members use their time. *Encourage families to divide chores between family members* by writing each chore on a slip of paper and putting the papers into a jar or box. Then have family members either work individually (or in pairs) to do family chores.

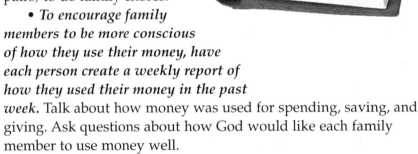

• *To encourage family members to be more conscious of how they use their money, have each person create a weekly report of how they used their money in the past week.* Talk about how money was used for spending, saving, and giving. Ask questions about how God would like each family member to use money well.

• *Develop an abundance offering for a month or during a specific church season.* Have children give one cent per toy or one cent per item of clothing. Some churches create a daily calendar that provides a stewardship challenge each day, such as "Give five cents for each pair of shoes you have." "Give two cents for each room you have in your house." "Give twenty-five cents for each bathroom in your house." "Give three cents for each friend you have."

• *Have families talk with their children about their money values in the spirit of abundance,* such as "we choose to spend our money in these ways or not to spend our money in these ways" instead of in a spirit of scarcity: "We don't have enough money for that."

• *Create an Advent calendar offering* where each child puts five cents into an Advent giving box or into a pocket of an Advent calendar during each of the twenty-five days of December. On Christmas Day, have children bring their Advent offerings to church.

Faith Discussion Take-Home Ideas

• *Have parents write a letter or be videotaped (or audio taped) as they tell about the details and feelings surrounding each child's birth.* (Encourage families to do this separately for each child.) For most families, the birth of a child, or the arrival of a child who is adopted, is a spiritual and emotional experience.

• *Discuss Sunday school lessons and/or the sermon on the way home from church* or during lunch following church.

• *Give each family a toy donkey, sheep, or some other animal from the Bible to use as an object for one family member to hide and the other family members to discover as they go about their day.* The object of this is not to play hide-and-seek but for a family member to place the item somewhere and for other family members to go about their day until someone happens to find the animal. Then that person brings the animal to the table for dinner that evening and tells where he or she found it. Usually a family discussion will occur. After dinner the person who found the item will hide the animal when family members aren't looking. Sometimes an animal can remain hidden for a number of days or even a week (which often causes family talking).

Often the animal shows up in the oddest place (such as falling out of the tube when a roll of toilet paper is changed or sitting in the sugar bowl). This often adds some humor to the family.

• *Post a map of the world on one of the walls of your house.* Paste a star on the countries where your church supports a missionary. Learn about these countries. Find out what the missionaries are doing and hoping to accomplish. Pray for the missionaries.

• *Go for a family walk near a lake or a nature center.* Or go for a walk through a zoo. Talk about God's creation.

• *Have families talk with extended family members about their faith journeys.* Ask questions, such as: At what point in your life has your faith been the strongest? Why? How did that impact your life? When did you feel you had no faith? What happened? What strengthens your faith most?

• *Acquaint families with words in Greek or Hebrew.* Find someone who knows Greek or Hebrew. (Often a minister knows someone who does, or contact a local seminary that may have a Greek or Hebrew scholar.) Have that person translate the first name of each family member in your church into Greek or Hebrew (and tell how to pronounce it). Have that person also give you the translation of Jesus in Greek and the translation of God in Greek and Hebrew. Often this information can generate discussions in families.

Family Worship Take-Home Ideas

• *With young children, have a church service at home.* Have children be ushers to collect the offering in baskets. Read a Bible story. Pray together. Sing hymns.

• *Focus on one hymn or Christian song each month* to learn the melody and the words.

• *Encourage families to find important dates of faith commitments,* such as baptismal dates, dedication dates (for traditions that have believer's baptism), first Bible receipt milestone, first Communion, confirmation, and other significant dates in your tradition. Have families mark the anniversaries of these dates by lighting a candle and talking about these important faith milestones.

• *Learn different songs that can be used as mealtime prayers,* such as "Praise God, from Whom All Blessings Flow" by Thomas Ken and "Come, Ye Thankful People, Come" by Henry Alford and George Job Elvey.

Notes

I. Family Ministry

1. The Alban Institute is an ecumenical organization that offers practical, research-based knowledge through publications, consulting, training, and seminars for people who care about congregations.

2. Roy M. Oswald and Speed B. Leas, *The Inviting Church: A Study of New Member Assimilation* (Bethesda, Md.: The Alban Institute, 1987), 54. The other two reasons are a "warm, welcome, caring community" and "meaningful worship and sermons."

3. Research statistics and quotes from Roberta Israeloff, "Finding a Spiritual Home," *Parents Magazine* 71, no. 12 (December 1996): 146-48.

4. Richard P. Olson and Joe H. Leonard, Jr., *A New Day for Family Ministry* (Bethesda, MD.: The Alban Institute: 1996) 38-39.

5. Oswald and Leas, *Inviting Church*, 54.

6. Ibid., 55.

7. Ibid., 58-59.

8. Ibid., 58.

9. Ibid., 72-73.

10. Ibid., 75.

11. Olson and Leonard, 82.

12. Diana R. Garland, *Family Ministry: A Comprehensive Guide*, (Downers Grove, Ill.: InterVarsity Press, 1999), 466.

13. Cindy Novak, "Who's Not Coming to Church," *The Lutheran* 14, no. 1 (January 2001): 34-35.

14. Ibid.

15. Roland Martinson, as quoted in Kathryn Christenson, "Breaking Open the 'God Box,'" *The Lutheran* (May 1997): 14-15. Martinson is a professor of pastoral care at Luther Seminary in St. Paul, Minnesota.

16. Ava L. Siegler, Ph.D., "What Kids Can Understand About God," *Child* 13, no. 3 (April 1998): 56-60.

17. Steven P. Shelov, editor-in-chief for the American Academy of Pediatrics, *Caring for Your Baby and Young Child: Birth to Age 5* (New York: Bantam, 1991), 286.

2. Program Basics

1. Eugene C. Roehlkepartain and Peter L. Benson, *Youth in Protestant Churches* (Minneapolis: Search Institute, 1993), 6, 117. The percentages cited do not add up to 100 percent due to independent rounding. The five mainline denominations included in the survey were the Christian Church (Disciples of Christ), the Evangelical Lutheran Church in America (ELCA), the Presbyterian Church (U.S.A.) (PCUSA), the United Church of Christ (UCC), and The United Methodist Church (UMC).

2. U.S. Census Bureau, *Statistical Abstract of the United States: 1999* (119th edition) (Washington, D.C.: U.S. Census Bureau, 1999), page 67, table 83. The percentages cited do not add up to 100 percent due to independent rounding.

3. Ibid.

4. Peter L. Benson and Eugene C. Roehlkepartain, "Single-Parent Families," *Source* (June 1993): 3, fig. 2.

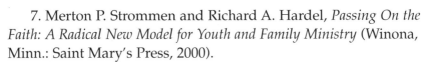

5. Roehlkepartain and Benson, *Youth in Protestant Churches*, 117. The percentages cited do not add up to 100 percent due to independent rounding.

6. Sarah Zimmerman, "Good men teach children's Sunday school," *National Christian Reporter*, 5 (September 1997): sec. A, 3.

7. Merton P. Strommen and Richard A. Hardel, *Passing On the Faith: A Radical New Model for Youth and Family Ministry* (Winona, Minn.: Saint Mary's Press, 2000).

8. Joan Huyser-Honig, "Forging Futures: Churches Offer People a Hand Up," *WKKF International Journal* 9, no. 1 (1998): 13-14.

9. John H. Westerhoff III, *Bringing Up Children in the Christian Faith* (Minneapolis: Winston Press, 1980), 89.

10. Peter C. Scales and others, *The Attitudes and Needs of Religious Youth Workers: Perspectives from the Field* (Minneapolis: Search Institute, 1995), 4, 15, 17.

11. Ibid., 15.

12. Peter L. Benson, Eugene C. Roehlkepartain, and I. Shelby Andress, *Congregations at Crossroads: A National Study of Adults and Youth in the Lutheran Church-Missouri Synod* (Minneapolis: Search Institute, 1995), 22.

13. *Family Works: A Publication of the Center for Ministry Development* (Naugatuck, Conn.: Center for Ministry Development, 1995). The Center for Ministry Development is a Roman Catholic organization that offers many resources

in family ministry. Contact the organization by writing to the Center for Ministry Development, P.O. Box 699, Naugatuck, CT 06770.

14. Eugene C. Roehlkepartain, *Building Assets in Congregations: A Practical Guide for Helping Youth Grow Up Healthy* (Minneapolis: Search Institute, 1998).

15. John Cook, comp., *The Book of Positive Quotations* (Minneapolis: Fairview Press, 1993), 483.

3. Exciting Education

1. Search Institute, *Effective Education: A National Study of Protestant Congregations, a Report for The United Methodist Church* (Minneapolis: Search Institute, 1990), 38.

2. Garland, *Family Ministry*, 470.

3. Roehlkepartain and Benson, *Youth in Protestant Churches*, 6, 110.

4. Joe Leonard Jr., *Planning Family Ministry: A Guide for a Teaching Church* (Valley Forge, Penn.: Judson Press, 1982), 12.

4. Service and Mission

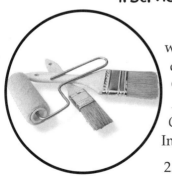

1. The other two are young people talking with parents about faith issues and family devotions. Source: Peter L. Benson and Carolyn H. Eklin, *Effective Christian Education: A National Study of Protestant Congregations* (Minneapolis: Search Institute, 1990), 38.

2. Ibid., 46.

3. Eugene C. Roehlkepartain, Elanah Dalyah Naftali, and Laura Musegades, *Growing Up Generous: Engaging Youth in Giving and Serving* (Bethesda, Md.: Alban Institute, 2000), chapter 7.

4. *Family Matters: The First Year* (Washington, D.C.: Points of Light Foundation, 1992), 40.

5. The "Desired Future for Families" statement of Family Life 1st, www.familylife1st.org.

6. "Family Volunteering Creates Meaningful Holidays," press release from the Family Matters program of The Points of Light Foundation, 1995.

7. *Volunteering and Giving Among Teenagers 12 to 17 Years of Age* (Washington, D.C.: Independent Sector, 1996), 2-40.

8. To date, only the Family Matters program of The Points of Light Foundation in Washington, D.C., conducts periodic research on family volunteering.

9. J. P. Hill, *Participatory Education and Youth Development in Secondary Schools* (Philadelphia: Research for Better Schools, ERIC Document Reproduction Services No. ED 242 701, 1983).

10. Robert Coles, *The Call of Service: A Witness to Idealism* (Boston: Houghton Mifflin, 1993), xxiii.

11. Roehilkepartain and Benson, *Youth in Protestant Churches*, 76.

12. *Family Matters: The First Year*, 48.

13. Marian Wright Edelman, *The Measure of Our Success: A Letter to My Children and Yours* (Boston: Beacon Press, 1992), 6.

14. "Baby Food," *The Lutheran* (March 2000): 39.

15. *Family Matters: The First Year*, 48.

5. Welcoming Worship

1. Benson and Eklin, *Effective Christian Education*, 49. The study included adults in the Christian Church (Disciples of Christ), Evangelical Lutheran Church in America, the Presbyterian Church, the Southern Baptist Convention, the United Church of Christ, and The United Methodist Church.

2. William H. Willimon, *The Service of God: Christian Work and Worship* (Nashville: Abingdon, 1983), 67.

3. Strommen and Hardel, *Passing On the Faith*, 161-62.

4. Philip S. Krug, "Teaching first graders how to worship," *The Christian Ministry* 29, no. 6 (November-December 1998): 5.

5. Donald Hinchey, *5-Minute Messages for Children* (Loveland, Colo.: Group Books, 1992), 5.

6. Benson, Roehlkepartain, and Andress, *Congregations at Crossroads*, 20.

6. Congregational Care

1. Olson and Leonard, *A New Day*, 65-66.

2. Benson, Roehlkepartain, and Andress, *Congregations at Crossroads*, 15.

3. Robert Wuthnow, *Sharing the Journey: Support Groups and America's New Quest for Community* (New York: Free Press, 1994), 170.

4. Benson, Roehlkepartain, and Andress, *Congregations at Crossroads*, 15.

5. Jim Larson, *A Church Guide for Strengthening Families* (Minneapolis: Augsburg Publishing House, 1984), 24.

6. C. Kirk Hadaway, *What Can We Do About Church Dropouts?* (Nashville: Abingdon Press, 1990), 41.

7. Olson and Leonard, *A New Day*, 65.

7. Music and the Arts

1. Roehlkepartain and Benson, *Youth in Protestant Churches*, 25.

2. Henry E. Horn, *O Sing unto the Lord: Music in the Lutheran Church*, (Philadelphia: Fortress Press, 1966), 4.

3. Michelle Burgess and Julie B. Sevig, "All grown up and ready for church," *The Lutheran*, 14, no. 1 (January 2001): 32-33.

8. Special Activities

1. Quoted in Melinda Blau, "Family Fun in the 90s," *Child* (March 1996): 86.

2. Karen S. Peterson, "Kids Saying to Parents: 'I Need You,' " *USA Today* (26 May 1987): 1A-2A, reported in *The Youth Ministry Resource Book*, edited by Eugene C. Roehlkepartain (Loveland, Colo.: Group Books, 1988), 32-33.

3. Jean Grasso Fitzpatrick, *Something More: Nurturing Your Child's Spiritual Growth* (New York: Viking, 1991), 142.

4. Alix Strauss, "Why You Need Less Work and More Play," *Family Circle* 111, no. 14 (October 1997): 56.

9. Take-Home Activities

1. Edelman, *The Measure of Our Success*, 6.

2. Ibid., 7-8.

3. Benson and Eklin, *Effective Christian Education*, 46-47.

4. Jennifer Norris Peterson, "Families as Faith-Builders," *The Lutheran* (May 1997): 16-19.

5. Fitzpatrick, *Something More*, 27.

6. Peterson, "Families as Faith-Builders," 16-19.

7. Benson, Roehlkepartain, and Andress, *Congregations at Crossroads*, 27.

8. Fitzpatrick, *Something More*, 47.

9. Benson and Eklin, *Effective Christian Education*, 46.

10. Leif Kehrwald and Rene Kehrwald, *Families Nurturing Faith: A Parents' Guide to the Preschool Years* (New Rochelle, N.Y.: Don Bosco Multimedia, 1992), 15.

Resource List

Organizations

Family Ministry organizations

Association of Family Life Professionals (AFLP)
3724 Executive Center Drive, Suite 155
Austin, TX 78731
(800) 393-8918
This nonprofit organization brings together church leaders, counselors, psychologists, lawyers, teachers, and any Christian who emphasizes the "basic need for Christ to be the center of all family life." It has a quarterly newsletter, a professional journal, workshops, an annual convention, and a national network of members.

The Center for Ministry Development
P.O. Box 699
Naugatuck, CT 06770
(203) 723-1622
cmdnet@mindspring.com
www.cmdnet.org
The Center for Ministry Development is a Roman Catholic organization that offers many resources in family ministry.

Family Ministry
Louisville Presbyterian Theological Seminary
1044 Alta Vista Road
Louisville, KY 40205-1798
family@femf.org
www.fmef.org
Published four times a year, *Family Ministry* is a mainline Christian journal that includes articles on family ministry, snap-

shots of congregations with family ministry programs, book reviews, and research findings.

National Marriage Encounter
(800) 828-3351
www.marriage-encounter.org
This national organization can connect you with Christian marriage encounter retreats in your area. Or contact the marriage encounter office of your denomination, such as the United Methodist Marriage Encounter (www.encounter.org), the Episcopal Marriage Encounter (www.episcopalme.com), or the Lutheran Marriage Encounter (www.ilme.org).

Prepare/Enrich Training
Attention: David Olson
P.O. Box 190
Minneapolis, MN 55440
(800) 331-1661
The University of Minnesota has created two couple inventories for churches to use: the Prepare inventory (for engaged couples who are going to marry) and the Enrich inventory (for couples who already are married). The inventories help couples talk about issues such as expectations, religious issues, sexuality, children and parenting, conflict resolution, communication, and roles.

Youth & Family Institute of Augsburg College
Campus Box 70
2211 Riverside Avenue
Minneapolis, MN 55454-1351
(877) 239-2492
www.youthfamilyinstitute.com.
The Youth & Family Institute of Augsburg College provides resources for family ministers (such as publications and workshops). In addition, it also publishes a 16-page Faithlife in the Home catalog that has resources for families to nurture faith in their children and teenagers at home.

Family Service organizations

Church World Service
28606 Phillips Street
P.O. Box 968
Elkhart, IN 46515
(800) 297-1516
cws@ncccusa.org
www.churchworldservice.org
Each fall, Church World Service sponsors an annual CROP
Walk for Hunger. This one-time walkathon event can appeal to all
kinds of families since the only requirements are to walk outside
on a weekend afternoon and ask for pledges for the family that
go to help hunger efforts. Families can pull young children in
wagons, push babies in strollers, have young children ride tricycles and bicycles while teenagers can walk along with the adults.

Family Matters
The Points of Light Foundation
1400 Eye Street, NW, Suite 800
Washington, DC 20005
(202) 729-8000
FAMILYMATTERS@pointsoflight.org
www.pointsoflight.org/familymatters
This program engages families in year-round community-
oriented volunteer projects. It also does research on family volunteering and sponsors an annual National Family Volunteer Day
each November.

Food Chain National Food Rescue Organization
(800) 845-3008
Have families volunteer to rescue food that's leftover at a special event, at restaurants, bakeries, and/or hospitals. Then have
families deliver the food to soup kitchens and homeless shelters
that serve meals. Often thousands of pounds of food go to waste
because food-rescue programs don't have enough volunteers to

help pick up the food and deliver it. To link up with a food rescue organization near you, contact this organization.

Global Village Department
Habitat for Humanity
121 Habitat Street
Americus, GA 31709-3498
(800) HABITAT, ext. 2549
gv@hfhi.org.
www.habitat.org

For families who like to travel and serve, Habitat for Humanity has the Global Village program. Families can travel to countries within Africa, Latin America, the Caribbean, Asia, and North America to build houses while also seeing the sights.

Group Workcamps
Box 599
Loveland, CO 80539
(800) 774-3838
www.groupworkcamps.com

If you're creating service projects for families with junior and senior high youth, consider going on a week-long workcamp through Group Workcamps. Each year, Group Workcamps offers close to fifty different workcamps throughout the United States.

Habitat for Humanity
121 Habitat Street
Americus, GA 31709-3498
(800) 422-4828
info@habitat.org
www.habitat.org

Habitat for Humanity has more than 1,700 affiliates in all fifty states, the territories of Guam and Puerto Rico and in sixty other countries around the world. Link up with a Habitat affiliate near you to do a family service project.

Make a Difference Day
1-800-VOLUNTEER
www. pointsoflight.org
Join USA WEEKEND's Make A Difference Day held on the fourth Saturday in October. Sponsored by USA WEEKEND and the Points of Light Foundation, the annual day of service helps churches, organizations, families, and individuals volunteer to make the world a better place.

St. Jude's Ranch
100 St. Jude's Street,
Boulder City, NV 89005
Ask families to keep greetings cards they receive for birthdays, anniversaries, and during Christmas. Have families come together and bring all their cards and see how many pounds of cards your church has collected. Send the cards to this organization where the children at St. Jude's recycle the cards to make new ones.

UNICEF
3 United Nations Plaza
New York, NY 10017
(212) 326-7000
www.unicef.org
Encourage families to do activities that also encourage children to give, rather than just receive. Some churches give children Unicef Halloween boxes where children also ask for coin donations when they go trick or treating. The Sunday following Halloween, children process forward during worship to place the Unicef boxes on the altar.

Volunteer Match
www.volunteermatch.org
Find service and mission opportunities near you by visiting this Web site, which allows you to post and find volunteer opportunities near you by typing in your zip code. The Web site has church-based and secular service projects for families.

Youth Service America
1101 15th Street, N.W., Suite 200
Washington, DC 20005
(202) 296-2992
www.servenet.org/ysa
Get families involved with National Youth Service Day each
April through Youth Service America, an alliance of more than
two hundred youth-serving organizations.

Family Ministry Books and Publications

family Ministry Resources

*Building Assets in Congregations: A Practical Guide for Helping
Youth Grow Up Healthy*, by Eugene C. Roehlkepartain
(Minneapolis, Minn.: Search Institute, 1998) presents a research
model of forty key factors (called assets) that children and youth
need to succeed. Chapter 6 of that book focuses on family ministry.

Family Ministry: A Comprehensive Guide by Diana R. Garland,
(Downers Grove, Ill.: InterVarsity Press, 1999) is the most comprehensive guide on family ministry available. Within the 627-page
book (which is an ideal textbook for seminaries and universities),
you'll find helpful information on the characteristics of strong
families, an in-depth section of biblical foundations for family
ministry, and ideas on how to plan and lead a family ministry.

*Family Works: A Publication of the Center for Ministry
Development* (Naugatuck, Conn.: Center for Ministry
Development, 1995) is a family ministry workbook that includes
family enrichment activities, parenting workshops, family learning activities, family rituals and celebrations, and family service
activities.

A New Day for Family Ministry by Richard P. Olson and Joe H.
Leonard, Jr. (Bethesda, Md.: The Alban Institute, 1996) examines
the trends of how families are changing and how the church can

best welcome different types of families, even when the church has theological difficulties with some of the decisions and issues these families are dealing with. This book is about how to make the church fit for families and how to be sensitive about diverse family issues.

Passing on the Faith: A Radical New Model for Youth and Family Ministry, by Merton P. Strommen, Ph.D., and Richard A. Hardel, D. Min. (Winona, Minn.: Saint Mary's Press, 2000) present a new model for doing youth and family ministry in this book. Not only does it address how to reach and keep families, but it also emphasizes the importance of the ministry churches provide for young people.

Family Service Resources

Beyond Leaf Raking: Learning to Serve/Serving to Learn by Peter L. Benson and Eugene C. Roehlkepartain (Nashville: Abingdon Press, 1993) is a comprehensive guide for engaging teenagers in service.

Teaching Kids to Care & Share by Jolene L. Roehlkepartain (Nashville: Abingdon Press, 2000) gives more than 300 mission and service project ideas for children age three to twelve.

Family Worship Resources

5-Minute Messages and More by Donald Hinchey (Loveland, Colo.: Group, 1998) features Bible-based children's sermons that really captivate children's attention and imagination. Donald Hinchey has written three other books of children sermons also published by the same publisher: *5-Minute Messages for Children* (published in 1992), *6-Minute Messages for Children* (published in 1993), and *5-Minute Messages for Children's Special Days* (published in 1994).

Children's Worship Bulletins—This Ohio company has weekly children's worship bulletins, one for ages three to six and another for children ages seven to twelve. Contact: CRI, 4150 Belden

Village Street, Fourth Floor, Canton, OH 44718; (800) 992-2144; www.childrensbulletins.com.

Forbid Them Not: Involving Children in Sunday Worship by Carolyn C. Brown (Nashville: Abingdon Press, 1993, 1994) shows how to create meaningful worship services that include children and families based on the Revised Common Lectionary.

family Support Resources

Helping Children by Strengthening Families: A Look at Family Support Programs (Washington, D.C.: Children's Defense Fund, 1992) highlights key ways to support and strengthen families.

Sharing the Journey: Support Groups and America's New Quest for Community by Robert Wuthnow (New York: Free Press, 1994) gives a comprehensive view of how to build community for people through support groups and other supportive groups.

family Arts, crafts, Music, and Drama Resources

100 Ideas for Music Ministry compiled by Mark Cabaniss and Phil Mitchell with Fred Bock, John Purifoy, and Bill Rayborn (Milwaukee, Wis.: Hal Leonard, 1998) tells how to build a stronger music ministry through this book and audiocassette package.

The Artist Way: A Spiritual Path to Higher Creativity by Julia Cameron with Mark Bryan (New York: Jeremy P. Tarcher, 1992) is a helpful resource to start a family journaling group that gets together to talk and journal.

Before and After Christmas: Activities for Advent and Epiphany by Debbie Trafton O'Neal (Minneapolis: Augsburg Fortress, 1991). This resource is packed with creative crafts to celebrate Advent, Christmas, and Epiphany.

Before and After Easter: Activities and Ideas for Lent to Pentecost by Debbie Trafton O'Neal (Minneapolis: Augsburg Fortress, 2001). The crown of thorns wreath on page 6 is especially creative and can give families in your church a way to mark Lent and the days of Holy Week.

Clown Ministry by Floyd Shaffer and Penne Sewall (Loveland, Colo.: Group Books, 1984) and *Clown Ministry Skits* for All Seasons (Loveland, Colo.: Group Books, 1990) give in-depth information and help in creating a clown ministry as a part of your family ministry.

Praising God Through the Lively Arts by Linda M. Goens (Nashville: Abingdon Press, 1999) gives easy-to-use ideas on how to use the creative arts (such as clowning, liturgical dance, and choral scripture reading) in worship services.

Family Special Activities Resources

Affordable Family Fun (Loveland, Colo.: Group Books, 1997) gives parents and church leaders fun, easy ways for families of four- to twelve-year-olds playing, talking, and laughing together. Each activity includes a Bible tie-in.

New Games for the Family (New York: Perigee Books, 1988) includes a large number of creative ways for families to play together and have fun.

Family Ministry Curricula

Family Rituals and Celebrations (written from a Catholic perspective) is a helpful resource to teach parents about the importance of family rituals. Have parents talk about the different family rituals they have and expose them to new family rituals. Contact the Center for Ministry Development, P.O. Box 699, Naugatuck, CT 06770; (203) 723-1622; www.cmdnet.org; E-mail: cmdnet@mindspring.com.

Five Cries of Parents by Merton P. and A. Irene Strommen (San Francisco, Harper & Row, 1985) is a book based in a Christian theology that easily lends itself to creating a five-series parenting class. Have a class on each one of the five cries: understanding, close family, moral behavior, shared faith, and outside help.

Time for Kids (which is available for educational purposes by calling 1-800-777-8600) has short articles in an eight-page format that are ideal for young people in fourth grade and older to comprehend and also easy for adults to read quickly. Teach and discuss current events and a Christian response to these events in an intergenerational class on faith and current events.

Total Family Sunday School (TFSS) is an intergenerational small group educational system that helps children, youth, and parents learn from each other, pray for each other, and create projects. It is developed by Rev. Richard Melheim, executive director of the Faith Inkubators Project, a Christian education systems think tank. Available from Faith Inkubators Project, (888)-55FAITH; info@faithink.com; www.tfss.com.

family Ministry Games

FaithTalk with Children (available from the Youth & Family Institute of Augsburg College, Campus Box 70, 2211 Riverside Avenue, Minneapolis, MN 55454; (877) 239-2492; yfi@augsburg.edu; http://youthfamilyinstitute.com) helps family members to talk about their faith experiences with each other.

The Ungame: Christian Version (available from Cokesbury at 1-800-672-1789; www.cokesbury.com) can be played with two to six family members ages five and up. This noncompetitive game encourages family members to talk about their faith and other issues.

Scripture Index

New Testament

Scripture Index